Leadership and Poverty

Ramaswamy Thanu

Printed by CreateSpace
An Amazon Company

Contents

About the Author

Ramaswamy Thanu (b.1934) obtained his Honors Degree in Economics from the University of Kerala and MBA from the Indian Institute of Management Ahmadabad. His experience embraces research, administration and management. In the early stage of his career he worked in the Reserve Bank of India and the Planning Commission, Government of India. He has published over thirty books. He writes books and articles combining humor, management and spirituality regularly .He is the Editor of two E Magazines –Enlightened Entrepreneur (Monthly) and Spiritual Ecology (Quarterly) published under the auspices of The World United.

4

Quotes

"So long as the millions live in hunger and ignorance, I hold every person a traitor who, having been educated at their expense pays not the least heed to them"

Swami Vivekananda

:"Generally the rich of the earth should prepare themselves for a simpler life in the future. The leading philosophy of the present, which always asks for more material goods and does not attach much value at simplicity of life or modesty in claims, has to be replaced by alternative philosophies. The real values of life do contain sufficient quantity of food and shelter; but it is not necessary to have the luxuries now aimed at. Cultural values will have to be upgraded again."

Prof.Jan Tinbergen
Nobel Laureate

"It is the failure of leaders in both developed and developing countries directly to address the problem of raising the quality of life that is the major cause of the fact that 800 millions of people are now in absolute poverty".

Robert McNamara,
former President of the World Bank

Preface

Poverty is a global phenomenon. In India we are living face to face with people in absolute poverty. The situation is depressing even after 60 years of India becoming a Sovereign Democratic Republic. Several measures initiated and implemented by governments, though laudable, have not made any serious dent on the problem.

It is the author's conviction that leadership has a great and critical role in elimination of poverty. The theme of the book is developed linking poverty and leadership. The conclusion derives strength and support from the statements of eminent men like Robert McNamara, former President of World Bank, Nani Palkivala, eminent jurist and many others. The inadequacy of strong, competent and benevolent leadership accelerates poverty by denying and depriving the benefits of economic growth to the poor. Corruption, power mis-management and break down of law and order are evidences of weak leadership at various levels.

Deeply concerned about the pitiable condition of the poor and the lethargy of leadership at many levels of government and outside, the author in all humility, outlines a programme of leadership development and social security for the poor.

The aim of the book is to plead before leaders, in all humility, to realize their role and to initiate positive and dynamic action for rapid economic growth in areas particularly relevant and beneficial to the poor. The example of a small country, Sri Lanka, in poverty alleviation, is of interest to those concerned with poverty alleviation and is given as an Appendix.

The author sincerely hopes that thousands of promising men in the country could be chosen for leadership training to serve a noble cause and for lasting results. The book may serve as an introduction to leadership development and an outline of an approach to the solution of the problem. Beyond this the author does not expect anything great to happen until the leaders assimilate the concepts and contents of the various chapters and act earnestly. If the target is well chosen, and the arrow fixed on the bow, the archer, assuming he is competent, releasing it will hit the target without fail. So for the best results the leader should be fully equipped, committed and trained. Such leadership alone can eliminate poverty.

T Ramaswamy
December 2015

Introduction

The problem of poverty dominates the discussions of all world leaders. Despite the rapid and amazing advance of science and technology the problem remains unsolved. Various measures are evolved and implemented by governments all over the world to manage resources effectively and realize the maximum benefits to the people badly hit by poverty. Every country wants higher economic growth. Material prosperity has come to be recognized as an important measure of a country's success. Similarly the capacity to command wealth is considered as the measure of individual's success. While the country wants to grow in terms of national income the individual wants to prosper by commanding more resources for a higher standard of living.

Government is increasingly resorting to economic planning for attaining economic growth. To achieve an egalitarian society more and varied measures are implemented. Spheres for development of industries are demarcated. Science and technology are harnessed for increasing the wealth and welfare of the community. Free education is provided to more people. Exports are encouraged to build up foreign exchange reserves. Various Acts are enacted in the legislature to regulate economic activity and to protect the weaker sections in the society. These efforts are supplemented by the contributions of international agencies like the World Bank and the Asian Development Bank providing technical and financial assistance.

Despite all these efforts the problem of poverty remains and poses a perennial challenge. The growth in national income and per capita income is rendered insignificant. It is often neutralized by inflation and a growing population. Some times the situation worsens due to the scarcity of essential goods and services.

Poverty exists at the individual and national level. When individual is the victim we call him poor. When a country witnesses the presence of a large number of such people we call it a poor country. The poor do not have the basic necessities of life viz; food, clothing, housing, education and health. They expect these to be provided by the government or some other agency. Those economically better off are in a position to provide such requirements themselves without direct government help. The latter can help anti poverty efforts in many ways.

Government is the fountainhead of power exercised through policies and strategies at various levels. Its role in a scheme of poverty eradication is to motivate the affluent people to transfer surplus resources to the poor and to provide the necessary administrative framework and infrastructure through legislative and executive action. Its important asset is power which has to be treated as a resource and used as a medium to influence the behavior of all other resources.

In a democracy the resource of power is vested in the elected representatives of the people and it takes various forms. It is exercised by the executive, legislature and the judiciary. While driving a car we know the power flow is regulated by coordinating the various functions discharged by the gear, clutch, accelerator, brake and the steering. Similarly the elected representatives of the people are expected to use the resource in a coordinated manner for the eradication of poverty. This is possible in two ways.

1.   Augmenting essential resources increasing their productivity and channelizing them primarily to meet the basic requirements of the poor and

2.   Conserving them. Conservation of resources is as important as augmenting them. In a large manufacturing firm it is easier to attain reduction in raw material costs which account for over 70% of the total costs in some cases, than to improve profits through increased output and sales. Similarly in a large country it is easier to conserve resources and to increase their productivity than to augment them. The key resource of power has to be conserved to augment and conserve other resources. This is the task before leadership. The failure of democracy to

make significant progress in the area of poverty abolition, despite various measures implemented, is due to the failure of leadership at all levels to conserve and channelize power and to use it to benefit the poor.

Thus the cure for poverty has to be found in the area of leadership. The various chapters in this book have this underlying theme and against this background the reader is requested to view poverty and the solution. Thus concepts like power management and development leadership have been discussed in detail. The incidence of rural poverty is more and towards improvement rural development with reference to poverty abolition is discussed.

The role of character in economic development assumes importance and greater reliance on value systems is advocated for building stronger foundations of economic progress. So this area is also emphasized for consideration seriously by leaders in power. A systems approach where formal and informal organization structures have to link their subsystems including voluntary agencies is considered necessary for poverty reduction. The example of Sri Lanka which has achieved significant progress in tackling poverty is relevant and is highlighted towards the end of the book.

1. Portrait of Poverty

Poverty is a state of being in want of the basic necessities of human existence. It presents a pitiable plight. The seriousness and depth of misery it inflicts on the victim is clearly understood if we focus our attention on individual poverty. When a nation lacks a system which ensures generation of adequate opportunities, output, productivity, employment, income, and distribution individual poverty raises its head.

Imagine a thatched hut located far away from a highway, housing a family of ten members, eight being children, four of them girls. The head of the family earns Rs 1000 per month during the work season and the average expenditure per head is Rs 100 per month. Four of the growing children discontinue their studies before completing the primary school stage. They cannot work even as servants as there is none within a walk-able distance to employ them. Two of them are ill. The other two are below four years.

The hut is leaky and threatens to collapse in the event of a heavy rainfall. The children are on the verge of becoming a victim to a serious illness. The family needs food for survival. Their present income will dry up when the work season ends. The situation is one of acute misery. The entire earnings of the family have to be used to postpone starvation. This situation paints an extreme form of poverty.

A sick man on a pavement is unattended for long periods. He does not have the strength to move or seek any remedy and thus remains there facing rough weather. Many look at him while passing by but few have any sympathy for him. This man is subject to extreme poverty. He is a citizen of the same society which consists also of many affluent individuals. In dire straits, being unable to draw attention and assistance, he dies as a result of starvation and malnutrition.

Poorly clad urchins are sometimes seen on a side walk rummaging through garbage collections in search of food left over by others. The desperate effort they spend on this process ends up as an exercise in futility. Apart from the unhygienic waste, society's apathy and toleration of such conditions is lamentable indeed. These unorganised victims of circumstances somehow continue to survive with rags on their backs and air in their bellies. Driven by uncontrollable hunger they often consume unwholesome food. Thus potentially healthy young men and women are turned into helpless crippled victims early in life.

Take the case of a mother with a baby in hand as well as in the womb, imploring the mercy of passers by. She is exposed to sun, wind and rain and there is no roof to protect her and her offspring. To hundreds of thousands of such human beings even pavements do not provide the berth for a few hours' rest. The absence of privacy forces them to lead a wretched state of existence.

The agony of a family of five with no certainty of the source from where the next day's food will come is frightening indeed. The sorrowful expression of such human beings cramped in an area of ten to fifteen square meters in a thatched improvisation resembling a pigsty is a painful sight. When the basic needs of food, clothing and shelter are not met ill health, ignorance and insecurity follow one another. Education, health and security are not present in their framework of thought when primary needs which keep body and soul together are not met.

Poverty leaves ugly scars on the victim. It inflicts malnutrition and in some cases serious illness. Education of children is ruled out for they have hardly any energy and resources left to think of utilizing free educational opportunities. Hygiene is totally absent. Even burning oil for lighting lamps at night becomes a luxury. Cultural development is zero. The family is under constant struggle and stress. This soon breaks the will of the members who ultimately resign themselves to their fate.

They begin to consider human existence as a burden and are haunted by thoughts of suicide. The impact of poverty is felt suddenly and severely when the breadwinner of the family dies or loses his job. When this source of income dries up his dependents face threat of starvation. The benefits of communication and knowledge do not come within their reach.

The poor are unable to command resources, which can give a better leverage for attaining higher standards of living. The force of circumstances compels children and adults to remain poorly dressed. The fortunate sections of society, who otherwise should have shown sympathy on them, generally look upon them with contempt.

As opportunities and other springboards of success elude them, the communication gap between them and the affluent sections widens steadily. Since any addition to their income is welcome, they send even children to work. The latter are deprived of the opportunity to acquire essential knowledge and skills, which are vital for a take off from poverty. The vicious circle of misery goes on widening, and many who trapped painfully look forward to the moment of deliverance though in vain.

A victim of poverty has no bargaining strength. Even if he produces something he has to sell it as distress sale due to lack of organization. In rare cases when a poverty stricken individual takes up a job on meager remuneration he undergoes unimaginable humiliation. His hatred for values and for the government tolerating such a social system deepens. He is lead by opportunists who use him as a lever to spearhead agitations sometimes bringing economic activity to a halt.

The focus of attention here is on the individual who is placed in the frying pan of trying circumstances. He is one among the millions of people below the poverty line who, according the Planning Commission, constitute over 27% of the Indian population. The continued existence of such large number of poor individuals in deplorable conditions shifts the focus of attention from the individual to the national level.

India's population in 2014 is estimated at 1.30 billion .In spite of family planning programmes the problem remains alarming. The country's population rose by 21.34 % during 1991 – 2001.It occupies only 2.5% of the world's land area, but supports over 15% of the world's population. Almost 40% of Indians are younger than 15 years of age. About 70% of the people live in more than 550,000 villages, and the remainder in more than 200 towns and cities. India adds almost the total population of Australia or Sri Lanka every year. The vast majority of Indians, nearly 74%, live in villages of less than 5,000 people. India is the home of one third of the world's poor; official estimates range from 26 to 50 percent of the more than one billion population.

In 2008-2009 the per capita Income in India was Rs 37490 which was very low compared to world standards. According to World Bank estimates 456 million Indians (41.6% of the total Indian population) now live under the global poverty line of US$ 1.25 per day. However, this also represents a significant decline in poverty from the 60 percent level in 1981 to 42 percent in 2005. As per estimates of the Planning Commission of India 27.5% of the population was living below the poverty line in 2004–2005, which was down from 51.3% in 1977–1978, and 36% in 1993-1994. A 2007 report by the state-run National Commission for Enterprises in the Unorganised Sector (NCEUS) found that 77% of Indians, or 836 million people, lived on less than 20 rupees per day. According to a recently released World Bank report, India is on its way to meet its poverty reduction goals. However by 2015, an estimated 53 million people will still live in extreme poverty and 23.6% of the population will live under US$1.25 per day. This number is expected to go down to 20.3% or 268 million people by 2020. The effects of the worldwide recession in 2009 have plunged 100 million more Indians into poverty than there were in 2004, increasing the effective poverty rate from 27.5% to 37.2%. The Indian economy has grown steadily over the last two decades. However its growth has been uneven comparing different social and economic groups, geographic regions, and rural and urban areas.

India currently adds 40 million people to its middle class every year. Analysts such as the founder of 'Forecasting International', Marvin J. Cetron writes that an estimated 300 million Indians now belong to the middle class; one-third of them have emerged from poverty in the last ten years. At the current rate of growth, a majority of Indians will be middle-class by 2025. Literacy rates have risen from 52 percent to 65 percent in the same period.

India was ranked 132nd in the UN Human Development Index in 2007-08. It is the lowest rank for the country in 10 years. In 1992, India was at 122nd place in the same index. The situation has become worse as per critical indicators of overall well-being. India has the highest number of malnourished people, at 230 million, and is 94th of 119 in the world hunger index, 43% of India's children under 5 are underweight (BMI<18.5), the highest in the world as of 2008. Though there has been a steady improvement in the general health of the population during the last 25 years, the picture we see today is dismal.

Millions of poor people still suffer from malnutrition. Very few enjoy a balanced diet. Medicines are costly and beyond the reach of many. Many hospitals are lacking in supply of essential equipments and medicines. The distribution of medical facilities in the country is uneven. The availability is inadequate even in urban areas. Hospitals are crowded and often essential medicines are not available in stock. With no financial resources the poor find it difficult to get timely attention and service which the illness deserves. Agitations and strikes disrupt and affect even such essential services.

According to the Medical Council of India, the allopathic doctor-population ratio at present works out to 1:1722. The ideal is a ratio of 1:500. Of these 80% of doctors practice in cities and towns, making the ratio 1:10000 in rural areas. Many people in rural areas live under insanitary conditions. Hazards to public health like mosquito menace, poor drainage, unhygienic drinking water, congested accommodation exist in many parts of the country including urban areas. After acquiring skills at great cost, heavily subsidized by the government, qualified doctors are compelled to work in poorly equipped government hospitals. Poor living conditions and inadequate infrastructure facilities discourage doctors from setting up practice in rural areas.

New York Times estimates that about 42.5% of the children in India suffer from malnutrition. The World Bank, quoting estimates made by the World Health Organization, states 'that about 49 per cent of the world's underweight children, 34 per cent of the world's stunted children and 46 per cent of the world's wasted children, live in India.'

Since the 1950s, the Indian government and non-governmental organizations have initiated several programmes to alleviate poverty. These include subsidizing food and other necessities, increased access to loans, improving agricultural techniques and price supports, and promoting education and family planning. Such measures have helped eliminate famines, reduce absolute poverty levels by more than half, and reduced illiteracy and malnutrition. The most important initiative has been the supply of basic commodities, particularly food at controlled prices, through the Public Distribution System as the poor spend about 80 percent of their income on food.

The poorest sections do not have adequate clothing. The hygienic consequences of this feature can be imagined. They are unable to protect themselves adequately from the ravages of extreme winter.

At the national level there are problems of survival, maintenance and growth. The main source of income is employment and according to published figures prices of many essential articles are soaring. This has become a frightening phenomenon. Though globalization of output and other resources has increased opportunities for employment, the inadequacy is still glaring. The resulting frustration manifests as agitations disrupting law and order causing wastage of resources.-both human and physical.

Millions of poor do not have any shelter and are exposed to the vagaries of nature. Many live in shelters resembling shacks built up of cast off materials. A large percentage of houses occupied by industrial workers in metropolitan cities are considered hygienically unsafe. Housing accommodation lacks ventilation and is congested. Often about ten persons are forced to live in a single room. There are many others who cannot afford even these facilities. Many people take to temporary shelter on pavements, railway platforms, bus stations and public monuments. Some houses in the villages are dilapidated. They face the danger of being washed away during heavy rains. The problem assumes serious proportions in the cities where unhealthy conditions prevail. Many live in shattered huts in the slums and several others do not have any roof over them.

According to 2001 Census 42.6 million people live in slums. This constitutes 15 per cent of the total urban population of the country and 22.6 per cent of the urban population of the states/union territories reporting slums.

The housing shortage for the country is estimated at 24.71 million units. The quality of housing in general is unsatisfactory. The living space is inadequate, unhygienic and cramped. In metro cities many buildings occupied by the poor are insecure. Unplanned construction of houses continues to occur. Building of housing units has lagged behind the demand. According to official figures shortage of houses has increased considerably. Construction costs and land values are going up, making it impossible for many to build and own houses. Yet no large-scale and sustained programmes are evolved and implemented for building cheap houses for the poor though liberal finance is made available through banks and other financial institutions.

Thirty two per cent of the people are still illiterate .The prevailing system of education is hardly conducive to the development of personality and character of the individual. These are essential ingredients of human excellence and vital for economic progress.

Strikes, agitations and closures have become a regular feature with many educational institutions. These are engineered by lower strata of leaders. This invariably reduces the time, energy and resources available for imparting education. Students, with exceptions, have become unruly and setting fire to government owned buses and property are not rare events.

Teachers are hardly any better. Often they launch agitations and strikes seriously damaging the cause of learning and discipline. These cause erosion of resources. Most students have little respect for the institution or teachers. Rarely do they try to imbibe qualities of discipline and harmony which used to be the fabric of healthy family and social life. Education, in general does not provide the necessary training to equip the individual to realize the purpose in life and to face challenges with courage and determination.

Poverty thus presents a painful picture. At the individual level it inflicts perpetual hardship and suffering. At the national level it manifests as shortage of resources and non availability of essential goods and services to the poor. Any attempt to identify the main cause for this situation takes us to the key factor of leadership which is critical for progress in the area of poverty alleviation.

Sixty years of democracy and economic planning have not ensured even the bare means of existence for the really poor. They do not have minimum levels of food, clothing, shelter, health and educational facilities. They are unable to pursue any form of worthwhile economic activity. Programmes of poverty alleviation have not yielded desired results since spiraling inflation eats away the real worth of the benefits.

Policies in the past often resulted in distribution of wealth and power in the hands of the richer classes, the politicians and the bureaucrats. These groups, with a few exceptions, use all means to corner wealth, privileges and power. While the already rich, privileged and organised classes of employees get compensation by way of increased emoluments and allowances the *really poor get nothing.* The benefits arising from the operation of the economic system are diverted in an increasing proportion towards the welfare of the already affluent sections. This trend is increasing and prominent with the advent of liberal economic reforms and globalisation.The case of the impoverished unorganized poor with meager or no income deserves immediate attention. This section of the population has to be provided immediate and constant relief to tide over the daily economic crisis. One can see a picture of misery and abject poverty while travelling along parts of Bihar and Orissa.

India' GDP in 2007 was US $1.09 trillion (approx. IRs. 4905000 crores). This works out as an average GDP per capita of $964(approx.IRs. 43380) Growth in 2007 was forecast at 9.2%. Growth was estimated to slow down slightly to 8.5% 2008. Despite rapid growth, poverty remains a real problem, especially in rural India. India faces the real challenge of making sure that all sections of the population continue to benefit from growth. Current estimates suggest that 27% of the Indian population live below the poverty line. According to published data 77% of

Indians live on less than half a dollar a day. Most of these low wages are in the informal sector, working in agriculture on doing odd jobs.

Government considered globalization as a first step to provide the lever for faster economic growth hoping this would benefit the poor. However, the results have not been significantly beneficial to the poor. Inequality has increased. Economic growth has been uneven. It has benefited only the skilled and wealthy, though disproportionately. Many of India's rural poor are yet to receive any tangible benefit from economic growth. More than 78 million homes do not have electricity. 33% (268million) of the population live on less than $1(Rs 45) per day. Moreover with the spread of television in Indian villages the poor are increasingly aware of the disparity between rich and poor. Eighty seven percent of the rural households do not have access to credit.

State ownership did not fulfill the aspirations of the poor. Though banks were nationalized, loans were given mostly to those already well off. Only recently micro finance has been made available. Poverty alleviation achieved only marginal success. Intermediaries and middlemen flourished. Government is settling problems of the already well off sections of people. Benefits of assets utilization in public sector go to the employees and consumers of the products, who can afford to buy. Profits siphoned off as bonuses again accrue to the employees who are already well off. Benefits of subsidized housing, health service, travel concessions, loans for purchase of vehicles or homes all go to the employees. These individuals are already affluent and far above the poverty line. The exclusion of 27% of those below poverty line is a serious omission in implementing policies and programmes for welfare.

Appointments of square pegs in round holes including ministerial berths bring about disappointing performance. Soft attitude towards corruption eats away considerable resources meant for the development of the public sector and the economy. Surplus manpower, delayed decisions, absence of timely information system, indiscriminate inventory build up and frequent changes in top management personnel affected performance of organizations meant for public welfare and poverty reduction. Striking workers are let off without any deterrent punishment in spite of loss caused to the organization and the nation. Technology up gradation has been slow. No doubt huge assets have been created through the public sector. But the really poor have been denied any share in the ownership of these undertakings. Another evil that eats away the fabric of democracy is corruption. The public and private sectors have been victims of corruption and this causes erosion of resources through unproductive channels. These resources are sometimes used for furthering the political ambitions of the party in power. This acts to the detriment of the poor. It is reported that in the construction industry alone 20% of the outlay leaks out through corrupt channels. This amount falls in the hands of those already well off who use this ill gotten wealth mostly for conspicuous consumption. A reasonable return of 12% on this amount could give a share of Rs.120 per individual below the poverty line. If we consider the multiplier and acceleration effect of this expenditure the returns should be several times. Actually this income should accrue to the really poor who are on the borderline of starvation.

It reflects badly on the functioning of the economic system that the affluent having regular income live in larger comfort and luxury. In addition they have access to power and influence which are used and misused to amass more wealth and privileges. While one class of citizens has too much for ostentatious consumption, the poor do not have even one meal a day. Loss of resources through corruption necessitates levy of taxes and imposition of duties which create inflationary tendencies.

The operation of the economic system is conditioned and contaminated by the influence of corrupt political elements. This creates and perpetuates vested interests and pressure groups in different strata of society. Those below poverty level remain where they are, facing further threat of falling into positions of insecurity and starvation. But the affluent sections with the help of vested interests promote their selfish goals, and divert and usurp the major benefits of economic development.

Ministers and political leaders command all power and wealth to fight elections perpetuating the vicious circle. Along with officials they show favoritism in appointments and postings. Workers enrich themselves with benefits at the cost of the organization and the poor. They do not allow the unemployed and the qualified to take up similar jobs. Doctors often prescribe unnecessary medicines and treatment. Engineers compromise on quality. Businessmen dilute quality and lubricate corruption ignoring ethics. Bank employees agitate for increased benefits and other privileges. Various lobbies with political connections exist .The list of vested interests goes on endlessly.

No government has been able to eliminate the dominance of vested interests despite proclaimed policies. These groups at different levels corner power and wealth to the detriment of the poor. They get votes on the plea that they are going to solve problems of the poor. But on assuming power they are busy looking after themselves safeguarding their positions. The motto of 'self before service' gains currency and is worshipped as a philosophy.

The service attitude is missing in the official machinery. What was considered as one's *duty* for which salary was paid has now come to be interpreted as a *service* or favour. For such a service reward in kind or cash is expected. Bureaucrats like to have control over little and often irrelevant details. Issue of a passport, sanction for a building, and allotment of land, ration card, release of payment towards goods supplied and release of cash subsidy are examples. Often these are not considered as a part of one's duty, for which salary is meant and paid. It is now deemed to be a service. The list is only illustrative. Vested interests rarely allow benefits to reach the poor. Instead they knock off the benefits exploiting the gullible poor.

The poor are not enlightened and organised to make their voice heard. They do not know what to ask for and how and are often reconciled to their fate. The attitude and actions of the organised working class work against the really poverty stricken people with little work. The management is helpless to enforce a decision in the best interests of the organization. Sectional interests and militancy push many others below the poverty line. No government has displayed the courage to demolish this evil. By show of organised strength affluent sections of workers and employees derive benefits of development.

Another instance is the practice of workers perpetuating and promoting poor work culture. Dozens of men are forcibly employed under union pressure to do a job. Such job does not exist or can be done speedily and economically by one man alone if given the freedom.

Industrialization and employment generation have not made a significant impact on poverty alleviation. Inadequate and infirm policies, labour militancy, unethical business practices, delayed decisions, worship of the motto 'self before service' and 'get rich quick' by all sections of society having access to income, wealth, influence and power, perpetuate the problem. Finance was meant to be used as a lever to enable the poor to command resources for self employment. In many cases the funds were siphoned off by the intermediaries and amount ultimately available to the applicant was less than 50%.

Projects which often failed and remained dormant for years are restored back to life only during election seasons. Politicians come up with populist schemes such as supply of food grains at very low prices, which have an overall adverse effect on the economy, as a substitute for employment generation. Poor illiterate masses are carried away by the schemes. Unemployment insurance introduced by a government provided for Rs.200 per month to each unemployed individual. This was given up for want of funds though it had limited coverage. In another case on assuming power pension for employees of a public undertaking was announced although the company had a cumulative loss of over Rs 200 crores.

With all these measures the problem of poverty continues to exist. Coherent national policy and coverage are lacking. Failure of programmes and loss of resources perpetuate the malady. The Above Poverty Line (APL) section of the population enjoys better living standards and brighter prospects. The higher the strata the larger the benefits and the leverage. The Below Poverty Level (BPL) section faces threat of starvation and suffers misery. Spillover benefits from investment and employment generation bring down the number of BPL individuals though not significantly.

Poverty thus presents a painful picture. At the individual level it inflicts perpetual hardship and suffering. Is it not a shame on us to tolerate and see this malady in our midst? Can we do anything at our level or collectively to eradicate it? Can we make a beginning to find a lasting solution? Can we improve the quality of leadership in all spheres of activity?

2. Leadership and Poverty

Leadership is the art of enlightening the masses making them realize what they *really* need in the context of *national interest* and persuading them to achieve by organising their efforts. At the root of all actions is thinking and the higher the quality of thinking the better the result of actions. This is an essential quality required for those occupying higher positions of responsibility and power in society and in government. Leadership at many levels lacks this quality of positive thinking. Current leadership activity if scrutinized will reveal that, barring exceptions, most of the time, effort, talent and other resources are devoted to solve problems other than those of the poor. This can be seen from daily newspapers in most parts of the country which carry little development news of relevance to the poor.

The lack of leadership is seen in the absence of a sense of proportion and perspective displayed by many strata of leaders. This distorts, confuses and conceals the real problems. National interests are often sidelined while sponsoring agitations. Unless a leader takes into account the constraints under which the government is operating he cannot develop a practical approach towards solution.

Over two thousand five hundred years ago Plato the Greek philosopher remarked that democracy died of a surfeit of freedom. In a democracy the son refuses to obey the parents, the student refuses to obey the teacher and the contagion spreads so that the horse begins to drive the wayfarer from the road. This view of Plato on democracy holds good today and is relevant when we examine leadership at various levels and of recent origin. The surfeit of freedom has pushed into positions of power human drainpipes that don't have any vision. They believe in the motto "self before service" and are not used to positive thinking for the ultimate benefit of society.

Leadership at various levels, barring exceptions, has not succeeded in inspiring the masses to excel or improve their performance in various fields of activity. It has failed to impart discipline in their attitude and behavior. The clamor for higher standard of living remains unfulfilled for millions. The spiraling inflation pushes those who come out of the poverty trap to fall into that again. The availability of essential goods and services is further reduced by strikes, lockouts and breakdown of law and order. Millions of man days are lost every year on this account alone. It is sad to note that such losses continue to occur even after realizing that over 27% of the population is below the poverty line. Non priority goods of no use to the common man and no relevance for survival are produced in large varieties and quantities. This is done under the banner of employment generation and demand fulfillment. They consume huge resources.

Large-scale agitations, organised by the potentially productive elements in the rural sector, reduce the availability of resources for increasing output of food grains. Violation of the principles of productivity and the damage caused through negligence, wanton destruction of crops and of the productive potential of cultivable land result in loss. Worsening law and order situation in some cases has proved to be a further deterrent to increase yield from lands. The ravages of nature such as drought and floods play havoc with crops. In some states demands of agricultural labour for higher wages have often been disproportionate to the yield, and the land owner's ability to pay .Many except those who have got land free, look upon ownership of cultivable land as a nuisance. They seriously attempt to sell the land or divert it for other uses. The Green Revolution has been encouraging to provide a solution to the food problem. Despite implementing land reforms and adopting modern techniques of cultivation, agriculture remains with sub optimum yield.

A feeling of general discontent exists among people which frequently results in breakdown of law and order. Strikes, bandhs and hartals cause huge loss of man days and output every year. Indiscipline is also evident in the behavior of many strata of leadership both in power and in opposition .Their statements give the impression that they are least concerned about national interest.

Rigid labour laws still exist and they deter enterprise. As an example firms employing more than 100 people cannot retrench workers without government permission. The effect of this discourages firms from expanding to over 100 people. Trade Unions have an important political power base and governments often shy away from tackling politically sensitive labour laws. By and large the position remains the same although exemptions are given to firms in the Information Technology sector.

In general the deterioration in the quality, content, and depth of leadership is reflected in the unfair means of handling problems and scams. Seldom does leadership point out the implications of the followers' actions, set definite goals or help the administration to preserve law and order. Political leadership at lower levels seeks strength and support of the masses by triggering conflicts from trivial causes. Contempt for law and order is widespread. Disregard for faith, discipline and hard work, key ingredients of success, makes the task of conservation and productive use of resources difficult. We need more resources to uplift the lot of the millions of poor above the poverty line. But the disrespect for law and order depletes the already scare resources thereby thwarting progress.

These leaders have learnt the wrong side of all philosophies with perversions. They are unable to inspire the masses with worthwhile lofty ideals. The leadership they provide sometimes foments trouble and results in death and destruction. They believe in objectives but these are based on self-interest. Of course, occasionally they reveal smattering of a few concepts in management and economics which they lavishly express during seminars.

Management by objectives according to them is fulfilling their own personal objectives. They do not have any commitment to productive resource utilization. Their actions result in wastage of resources. Examples are many. Destruction of public property during agitations is one such instance. They believe in management by nuisance. The target for nuisance is the public and others who do not come within their party fold.

The large and growing population in the country always and at short notice facilitates command of an army of unemployed youth. They are professionally trained in trouble making and available on hire. The leaders use them as a tool for spearheading agitations, disruption of all economic and business activity creating impediments to normal life, processions blocking traffic, preventing flow of essential services, demonstrations and lightning strikes. Patients critically ill are unable to reach the hospital for treatment. If the same persons engaged in destructive and restrictive activities were to devote so much time for growing bananas it will earn foreign exchange worth several million dollars.

The inconvenience to the public caused by the champions of this philosophy of *management by nuisance* is great. Tourists and passengers arriving from distant places by rail, road, or air are stranded at the airports, rail and road terminals. With fatigue writ large on their face the travelling public wait for some mode of transportation for hours. We are familiar with the concept of management by crisis. That does not cause as much damage and agony as this practice of management by nuisance.

Nuisance assumes many forms. Imagine a group of miscreants encircling an official for hours even denying the facility of using the toilet or having food. This epidemic has grown to enormous proportions. Leaders who organize such agitations find justification saying that it is a democratic way of protest.

They create work for the police, which find its manpower deployed for various jobs other than for discharging the prime responsibility of maintenance of law and order and prevention and detection of crime. Repeat performance of these practices often results in violence. More work is created for the police and for the judiciary. This results in a non-functioning government where the executive, legislature and judiciary are forced to do unimportant work outside their normal duties. Even when the officials want to act their leaders in power do not give them support unless it suits their interests and convenience.

Poverty breeding elements emerge and gather strength in an environment where people's needs are growing fast out stripping resources. If needs are allowed to multiply and existing resources are wasted or used unproductively, poverty finds a safe berth to park itself.

Non availability of adequate quantities of goods and services to satisfy the basic wants of individuals at reasonable prices has pushed many towards the poverty line. The effects of the worldwide recession in 2009 have plunged 100 million more Indians into poverty than there were in 2004. Rising prices of essential commodities curtail the purchasing power of the poor and invariably their health, education and shelter needs are sidelined.

The trend towards increasing employment without adding to productivity causes the operation the law of diminishing returns. Unproductive employment benefits neither the individual nor the society. Such persons find enough free time to launch agitations and prevent others including those productive, from doing work. They block resources otherwise available for more important purposes and generate conditions which strengthen the cause of poverty .There is no convincing evidence to suggest that by and large leadership at many levels is becoming intensely aware of implications of the measures advocated and implemented.

In general political leadership holding sway over the organised masses above the poverty line succumbs to pressures. Often this action results in ignoring the interest of the unorganized labour whose strength is many times than that of the organised labour. The already well of sections in society, particularly in public service, manage to get additional benefits. Thus substantial share of the available resources is diverted towards providing benefits to a small section of people who are far above the poverty line. The frequent upward revision of salary and dearness allowance of government servants is an example. This reveals myopia of leadership reducing the availability of resources for the poor.

Absence of leaders with missionary zeal limits the extent of availability of resources, equitable distribution and the impact of assistance under various community welfare programmes. The affluent sections of society manage to get a substantial portion of the benefits from community welfare measures. Low quality leadership organising such efforts at lower levels renders such measures ineffective. Shady, shaky and stunted leadership and inadequate welfare measures perpetuate poverty.

Vested interests exist at every stage usurping large benefits of economic development and from the welfare measures of the government. In various areas of activity they gain command over resources otherwise available to the poorer sections of the population. They harass the latter and even seek illegal gratification for rendering any such service. At many levels officials do not have the necessary delegation and authority required for effective discharge of responsibilities. Each group is clamoring for rights and privileges without justification and regardless of the long term implications of their actions. Decisions taken are piecemeal and delayed. In business and commerce many men make their positions secure by high profiteering. They charge high consumer prices and supply substandard products. The presence of corrupt officials helps them in attaining these undesirable objectives.

The government's soft attitude towards corruption worsens the situation of poverty. Ministries undergo change and the promise of rooting out corruption is again held out to the electorate. Many ministers occupying cabinet positions get dislodged on grounds of promoting and participating in corruption. Some are forced to resign. Later an enquiry commission is set up which works at a great cost to the exchequer. A few years later reports are submitted. In some cases charges are never established .In others charges are proved but the new government decides to drop all action against the corrupt men. The reports are shelved till the opposition which promised action comes to power and takes up the cases. In the process it also becomes corrupt and goes underground on more severe charges. Ultimately the corrupt elements escape unpunished. All they have bequeathed is poverty and inequality because they have usurped the resources in varying degrees through various scams.

Efficiency in organizations requires good policies. These serve as guidelines for others at lower levels to follow and act. Policy making is the task of the highest executive. The benefits to the public from such policies depend on the competence of the leadership in authority and the clarity of ethics based objectives. In government policy making at the highest level can bring good for the people or spell disaster.

Professionally managed organizations and governments evolve sound policies beneficial to the people. Yet many governments lag behind in efficiency and transparency. The highest policy making body is the secretariat. Here all ministers and top executives have offices, opportunities for mutual consultations, discussions and conferences. It turns into a hub of competence or incompetence depending on the perspectives of those who formulate policies.

If the political executive gives importance to induct professionalism in administration policy making becomes sound and beneficial. Professionalism has built in advantages. There is respect for time, emphasis on fast and sound decision making, training of personnel to attain maximum efficiency and the commitment to serve the people. The lower strata in administration also take the cue from the top and try earnestly to be competent and adopt a professional approach to problem solving.

In contrast we have governments where the policymaking body, the secretariat, which is the hub of governmental activity, becomes the *hub of incompetence* and a den of corruption. This is so when politicians are pushed into positions of power by unfair means and have tainted records devoid of professionalism and values.

Often such politicians come to power through corrupt means and by making hollow promises to the people. While in power they carry with them the traits of acting unprofessionally, obliging faithful followers with favors. They sit on a volcano of tainted money waiting to be laundered. They give a free play to their greed and corner resources for themselves and for loyalists.

Corruption originates from the hub of incompetence. It abdicates ethics and good principles of management. It causes delays and harassment of people for rendering various services, otherwise legitimately due. They pass on the benefits down the line inducing them to devise ingenious ways and means to multiply and amass ill gotten wealth. Poor performance is a guarantee under such a set up. The public visiting the hub have nothing but a feeling of disgust. The result is spiraling inefficiency. There is competition in mediocrity. Unless the key leadership is overhauled with drastic changes by a powerful leader or public opinion the hub develops more networks to spread its tentacles of Incompetence. The hub of incompetence is the bane of society. Only strong enlightened public opinion can reverse this trend.

Corruption is not confined to a section of politicians or the civil servants alone. Private industry and commerce also contribute their share. Stress on industrialization opens up avenues for quick money making. The cumulative effect of corruption is the build up of black money which in India during 1948 to 2008 is estimated at over Rs 20 lakh crores. The amount is nearly 40% of India's gross domestic product, and nearly 12 times the size of the estimated loss to the government because of the 2G spectrum scam. The study was conducted by Global Financial Integrity, a non-profit research body that had crusaded against illegal capital flight. Dishonest industrialists, scandalous politicians and corrupt officers are reported to have deposited large amounts in foreign banks in their illegal personal accounts.

This amount has been appropriated from the people of India by exploiting and betraying them. Once this amount of black money and property comes back to India, the country's foreign debt can be repaid fully .Yet we will have surplus, almost 12 times the foreign debt. If this surplus amount is invested, the interest will be more than the annual budget of the Central government. Even if all the taxes are abolished, the Central government will be able to maintain the country comfortably. Black money functions as a parallel economy diverting resources, pushing up prices and perpetuating poverty. The increase in corruption propensity of officials foils the attainment of 'power objectives' of the government.

Management seeks to attain definite objectives often with inadequate resources. Several concepts, tools and techniques have been evolved and practiced. But these techniques fail and surrender before a technique, which succeeds remarkably well. This is not taught in any B school, but widely practiced underhand. It is the technique of bribing. There are several ways in which bribe operates. We can take the example of cash payment. Where established techniques fail bribe succeeds. Bribing spreads its tentacles in all areas of economic activity .It has a comprehensive coverage. People in all walks of life sometime or other face this demon. It overpowers many. Often it is a hefty phenomenon filling deep pockets and large suitcases. Businessmen invariably keep this in their armory when all other techniques fail to get results. Even a simple decision without any favour invites bribe just because of the powerful position held by decision maker. Without this the decision will not be forthcoming or it will be unfavorable. We will consider an example where all professional techniques failed and bribing succeeded.

A large company faced a strike situation, which they wanted to avert. The dispute was over salary revision and bonus payment. Negotiations went on for two weeks. The stalemate continued. The best human relations expert was brought. He analyzed every bit of information and negotiated presenting all facts. But the unions refused to be convinced and turned down the proposal. Then as a last resort some one suggested to try the *hidden technique* from the armory. He said, 'you bribe the union leader. You will succeed and the strike will be called off.' The management heeded the advice. Negotiations with the leader took place. These were confined only to the rate to be paid to him and not any of the technicalities of the agreement or wage revision. The leader gave a compromise formula which worked. The management was surprised. They had originally agreed to pay more but the unions were adamant and did not accept. Now even considering the bribe paid to the leader as a cost the total financial commitments were less. Not only this, the strike was called off. So bribing succeeded when expertise failed.

Ultimate success in such an environment depends on how one succeeds in this game of bribing. Those who cling on to core competence and ethics will be drowned in the sea of bribes, which make organizations float, navigate and succeed. It is greed that foments and breeds bribe. When the question was raised before a CEO of a large Company, he said, 'My dear Gentleman, you have to treat it as cost.' Of course it is hidden cost and a technique too!

Power is often used to grant favors or to create and protect vested interests. Corruption is rampant in an environment where no control exists on the exercise of power. It is fuelled by a leadership which permits such an environment to prevail without devising effective measures to counteract the adverse influences. It manifests where performance is not measured. The existence of many 'power centers' without coordination or authority, together with imbalance in power distribution, results in ineffectiveness. This causes power leakage. The main 'power centers' become powerless even if they are manned by men of integrity, zeal and talent. They become ornamental designations. Power is misused and erosion takes place by force of circumstances together with legislative action or inaction .That power which should have been used by the government for a national cause is diluted or misused even when a business man is threatened with murder by workers during a strike. Power thus leaks out and reaches those who pose a menace to industrial progress and work against national interests.

Usurping resources by organised sections of society brings denial of opportunity to the unemployed. The former corners influence and resources with which they easily counteract any move by the unorganised sections. By this action resources are not made available to the deserving people. Corruption causes erosion of resources and inequality of incomes. It is the mechanism which converts power vested in the government for enriching the holders' own status or increasing wealth at the cost of service to the public. The power vested in an official is a governmental resource. It has been estimated that the loss to the nation by way of corrupt practices in the construction industry alone is 20% of the total outlay.

Permitting a privileged section of people to get higher remuneration without corresponding increase in productivity is not a *healthy* way to ensure equality. An egalitarian society will remain a dream if an organization is compelled to pay a bonus of 50% due to intimidation and pressures exerted by a section of the labour force. The support for such a bonus, provided by the conciliation effort of the government reduces the availability of resources for the benefit of the unemployed. It is surprising that the idea of mobilizing bonus in excess of 20% and adding it to government revenues to utilize it for further productive investment is not seriously considered and used as a means of mitigating poverty.

In a poor country opportunity the most important factor required to develop one's talents and capabilities, is lacking. Those already in the higher income group command more resources and gain influence through direct and informal exercise of money power. Others who are left behind in the struggle for improving standards of living have strength of numbers. These two forms of power clash in all areas of economic activity. The government is vested with the power to minimize the conflict between the two power groups having the power of wealth and the power of numbers. But it has not achieved significant success in this direction. Population growth and inflationary pressures in the economy push many more into the second category.

The problem of inequality is not really that of income and wealth distribution. It is the inequality of opportunity. The beneficiaries are those who champion the cause of the poor. They hold high positions in society and aspire for higher levels of leadership. Their actions are watched by many. Others follow their practices and a perverted concept of success and practicality develops among the followers. Talented individuals sometimes get opportunities to launch and promote productive ventures which help to boost up employment and output. But they are unable to ward off pressures from vested interests to protect themselves and to enrich their contribution to society.

The power potential of the government is not realized through effective 'power management'. In a democracy power is transferred from the people to the organs of government viz., the executive, legislature and the judiciary. These institutions are power generating and power balancing mechanisms. The inequality in distribution of power among these organs and their exercise can have serious effects on the quality of democracy.

Another form of inequality which is equally important is the inequality arising from the actions of organised sections of society. The magnitude and urgency of this is not analyzed and understood. They have secure jobs and incomes varying from 5 to 40 times of the assumed income requirements of those at the poverty line. Yet they agitate and snatch away from the government and employers enhanced rate of bonus, dearness allowance, and similar benefits. The benefits usurped every year come to over Rs. 2000 crores .When millions of unemployed exist resources raised mainly benefit those already affluent. This could be justified if there was any corresponding commitment on the part of the same recipients to increase production and productivity. Such commitment is seen only to get more such benefits at regular intervals.

Privileges for individuals and officials by virtue of their importance in society irrespective of their own contribution continue to exist. With the increase in the number of such people and their clout they obtain more privileges. Their actions result in diversion of resources for the benefit of those already affluent .Privileges cause a shift of resources from the needy to the affluent classes. The prominence of the latter makes others clamor for privileges as a status symbol. This brings inequality without adding to productivity.

The affluent resourceful classes in general, have not acted according to their financial strength and capability to alleviate poverty. This is seen in the luxurious ways of living and the waste that is part of their life. A Rs 7000 lunch or dinner in a star hotel for a single individual is an example. Their resources have not been put to the best use for the common good. Nobody denies the need for incentives for entrepreneurship and motivation. But there is no justification for displaying one's vanity by pompous ways of living when millions are struggling for a substandard meal. The privileged class also includes that category of leaders who claim to champion the cause of the poor. Their actions usually bring the opposite result of stifling productivity and promoting poverty. Having established their leadership in key positions they practically forget the poor and seek to serve only sectarian interests.

The enthusiasm and earnestness seen during a strike or a rally mobilizing thousands of people is not seen in organising or supporting any productive venture. The diversion of human and material resources for such activities is unjustifiable. The resulting waste is wanton and colossal. In no way they contribute to mitigate poverty. Often leaders whip up needs without educating or persuading people to change their attitudes. Leaders at many levels rarely act in the national interest. Instead they champion the cause of those making exorbitant demands.

Value systems contribute to the existence or removal of poverty. The individual has a growing need hierarchy whipped up by the exhortations of leaders. Contemporary ways of living suitable to the rich encourage indiscriminate borrowing by many. Absence of a dynamic value system brings disregard for human beings in general and the poor in particular. Selfish interest dominates.

Values provide a strong base for people to cooperate and support one another during emergencies consistent with availability of resources. They act as an informal system of built-in social security. The deterioration in the content of the value system considerably weakens anti-poverty orientation to the nation's efforts. Any socialistic programme launched by a government cannot succeed and endure without the support of basic values conducive to harmonious living. Values act as stabilizers and help to change attitudes in the interest of society. There have been superficial attempts to change the attitudes of people without getting them committed to basic values of life.

In a country with a growing population with inadequate material resources with the government having limitations, a rich value system has anti-poverty orientation. This has not been tapped and used as an intangible resource. High regard for values by leaders in particular can inactivate the poverty breeding mechanisms.

When a law and order problem turns serious and deaths result 'power management' fails. The 'power centre', the police, does not have the strength to neutralize the strength of the agitators. It is aware of the obstacle potential of the situation but lacks the motivation to use power effectively. There is no power objective at any level of the power hierarchy in consonance with national interests. Without clear power objectives the various 'power centers' are at best a mass of ineffectual individuals .The higher levels do not review the needs of 'power centers' and attempt to support by timely actions. The 'power centers' below are not strengthened by identifying the deficient areas seeking power from other sources like the legislature. In the power network the 'power centre' handing the situation is directly responsible for controlling the actions of the law breakers. It has equal responsibility to exercise power before the power breaking obstacle develops into a formidable threat. This aspect is often ignored by those in power. The result is that the power breaking mechanism gains strength and ultimately sweeps away the power hierarchy making it ineffective. The 'power centre' fails to enforce discipline. Its failure shows that a potential threat to power maintenance is developing.

This 'power centre' does not acquire power when badly needed, by seeking it from the top layers of the administration. Nor does it seek through legislative action for support. It is not easy to get such assistance since all members of the ruling party may not support the move of the government. This is difficult with a coalition cabinet with parties having diverse interests. There are limitations arising from the reluctance of the government to displease a section of the people. It implies that the 'people's will' vested in the government is not effectively used to reinforce the power mechanism to serve the national interest.

Effective exercise of power at the 'power centre' closest to the scene of action depends on many factors. These are the competence of the agency holding charge of the position, the power flow or support given by the 'power centers' above and the speed with which this is done. The top layers of the power mechanism have their roots in the party and the people. As long as solution to this ineffectiveness is not found at the root level power mis-management will continue to occur. Also the power structure will steadily weaken. Consequently obstacles to elimination of poverty and unemployment will strengthen and multiply.

Where the government is wedded to the concept of a welfare state with over 27 percent of the population below the poverty line, power mismanagement will perpetuate poverty. It prevents proper distribution of income. The conditions for increase in employment are not generated and sustained. Prices rise and inflation threatens the existence of the poverty stricken people. Productivity declines and vested interests develop at critical points thwarting the implementation of anti poverty programmes. Distorted power structure results in stalemate and retards progress in many areas of economic activity. Corruption gathers momentum and considerable leakage of resources occurs.

Generally leaders emphasize what is *wanted* by the people and not what is *actually needed* by them in the context of *national interests*. The situation is akin to one where a patient lying on an operation table expresses the fear that it is his first operation and the doctor tries to infuse confidence announcing that it is his first operation too. Often the representatives of the people arc placed in a position in which they profess to be leaders of the people while playing the role of followers all the time. Leaders rarely succeed in shaping public opinion based on relevant facts.

The elected candidates are expected to discharge their duties to the people. Here again often it is the caliber of the representative that determines effectiveness. Considerable time is devoted to unimportant squabbles and issues losing sight of priority problems. When jobs are needed for millions emphasis is given to national debates on trivial matters like surveying the toilets in the country or inquiring into corruption in the previous cabinet. There is no sense of proportion and direction. Important problems remain buried and unsolved. Economic development suffers and entrepreneurs are scared to invest.

Legislature devotes time for discussing trivial issues. The sessions are infrequent and the duration short compared to the need for deliberations of bills. Legislature, at times, presents a human version of a zoo. The theory of animal behavior without control fits in here. Undisciplined behavior of members is widely brought to the public view through live telecasts. Still the public does not learn and act. It is a sad state of affairs. A time utilization study of members in the legislature and of their contribution would reveal a disappointing performance. The privileges enjoyed by the members do not permit this attempt in most cases.

They are a privileged class who are not bound by any law except the one relating to their salary and perquisites, which they always want to be hiked. Rarely problems are discussed with a national perspective giving importance to seriousness, urgency and growth trend.

In a poor country with lot of unemployment, poverty alleviation and employment generation do not receive adequate attention and action. Exceptions occur during elections when the manifesto speaks about these but the authors soon forget.

In the legislature the conduct of the members is deplorable. Many scenes from the live telecast of proceedings of the state and central legislative bodies lend support to this view. Several days are lost without transacting any business   thus causing loss amounting to crores of rupees. It is reported that recently 23 days' of stalling proceedings in the Parliament is estimated to have cost the exchequer Rs. 170 crores. The legislature was adjourned continuously for 23 days. Statements by leaders raise doubts about their concern for national interests.

 Opposition leaders often aim at placing obstacles before the government while implementing programmes. Colossal waste occurs for want of skill on the part of the leadership to minimize it. Leakage of resources, lack of firmness on the part of administration, mid term elections, floor crossing, engineered ministerial instability, judicial enquiry etc. continue to occur. Power seeps into areas where it weakens the power mechanism. It foils attempts to maintain law and order. Thus energies of the masses are misdirected. Often the contribution resulting from such leadership becomes a monument of misdirected energy.

The immense power of leadership for the deliverance and progress of the nation is seen in the achievements of leaders like Mahatma Gandhi. He aroused a nation of 400 millions to work for the attainment of freedom. Barring exceptions leaders have not been successful in taking quick corrective action. Gandhi aroused the people's will for reaching a supra ordinary goal and the Indian masses responded splendidly. Such a response was seen to a great extent during the Indo-Pak conflicts of 1965 and 1971 under the leadership of Lal Bahadur Sastri and India Gandhi respectively. It is sad to note that only a crisis like war can bring out the best in the people .The present Prime Minister, an eminent economist, is steering the Indian economy towards higher rate of economic growth. But many at the lower levels do not rise to his vision and integrity.

Leaders, both in government and outside, have not used the antipoverty weapon of *social discipline* for reducing the loss of man days and output. In 2010, five million man days were lost. A 50% reduction in the number if avoided could help to achieve at least 2% increase in national income. With a proper system of income distribution thousands of people could be lifted out of the poverty net.

Leadership has been breeding and strengthening conditions which work against real progress. Energies and talents of many in a position to do good for society are frittered away due to hostile conditions generated by faulty leadership. Problems get more complicated because of delayed actions of leaders and their inability to see things in the proper perspective. There is no attempt to form a *think tank* consisting of talented men and women, as in some countries, to advise leaders on right lines about problems of constituencies.

The task of leadership is to help development of available resources according to priority curbing ostentatious ways of living. Leadership at various levels ought to be engaged in the task of balancing needs and resources of the nation. But it has been causing wastage of resources. The problems in areas discussed earlier i.e., production, productivity, employment, income, vested interests, corruption, inequalities, privileges, opportunity, resources, needs, value systems, 'power management' etc. are only symptoms of the more basic cause - that is poor leadership.

In short we don't have as many *problem solving* leaders as *problem creating* ones. The predominance of the latter is so great that the work of the former is neutralized and rendered ineffective. Many problems remain unsolved and some become chronic because of the acute shortage of leaders who fit in with the right definition of leadership. Most of them come under the category of leaders who follow. It is necessary for us to reverse the trend. This takes us to consider the task of setting anti poverty objectives.

3. Anti-Poverty Objectives

It is a most distressing feature that in India over 27% of the population lives under conditions of extreme poverty. Affluent citizens will have to think seriously of these unfortunate people and do something to improve their lot with reference to the framework of objectives for poverty elimination outlined below.

The growing gap between needs and resources compels us to realize the necessity to conserve and increase the quantum of resources and to curtail the needs of the affluent people consistent with anti poverty objectives. This must be the national objective of the government. The emphasis should be on providing increased income for the poor. Leaders in power, outside and in the opposition and at various levels have the responsibility to see that their actions positively support the following objectives. These are explained below.

1. To reduce the rate of growth of population

This helps to achieve balancing of needs and resources. This can be done by curtailment of needs without allowing them to grow in variety and magnitude. This will also reduce the pressure on resources for poverty abolition. Gradually the country will reduce unemployment and per capita income will rise. Law and order problems will be more manageable. Improved standard of living will reduce the mania for agitations and the additions to the army of agitators.

Governments will have to increase financial resources selectively by higher rates of taxation, direct as well as indirect. This will reduce inflationary pressures and maintain price levels by reducing the availability of money supply. The chances of internal peace will be better and citizens are less likely to be discontented. To attain this basic objective, the people's attitudes, which retard national growth, have to be changed. This can be done through persuasion by all levels of responsible leadership. Otherwise the gap between promise and performance widens and agitations increase in variety and number.

2. To increase output and services in all areas of economic activity considered vital for the survival of the people.

Poverty elimination and balanced economic development require a system of priorities according to which goods and services essential for survival are produced in large quantities. When basic needs are met, discontent subsides. Governments will have more time for productive activities. Law and order problems will be less. People develop confidence in the government and they easily understand the intentions of the administration.

Such a scheme of priorities helps to conserve resources and ensures that low priority needs are not met. It also helps to develop an attitude of austerity on the part of the affluent classes. They realize that non- essential items are not easily available.

3. To increase productivity in all areas of economic activity

This can help to provide an effective answer to the problem of poverty. Emphasis on productivity ensures a higher rate of output for a given quantity of input and thus the best results from available resources. Realization of this objective brings increase in output in all sectors of the economy. This helps to stabilize price levels.

The phenomenon of too much money chasing too few goods will be within manageable levels. The standard of living of the masses improves. It becomes easy to adopt improved technology and know-how. The general attitude of the citizens undergoes favorable change.

Reduction of unit costs in major areas of manufacturing and commercial activity becomes possible. This acts as an incentive to employ more factors of production and in this process employment increases.

To facilitate the attainment of this objective the system of education needs to be reorganized with anti poverty orientation. The quality of leadership at all levels needs improvement, stressing the need for respect for facts and to shift the emphasis from creating problems to solving them. Managerial skills have to be developed at all levels. Only those privileges that is productive, essential for protocol reasons and supporting anti poverty objectives need be provided and perpetuated.

4. To ensure that the major part of the increase in national wealth accrues to the people below the poverty line.

A Welfare State has to look after the needs of the weaker sections of the community. In a country where such population exceeds 27 percent of the total, it is only legitimate that they are given more attention and resources by the government. Any system of economic planning must ensure that the major part of the additional increase in national wealth accrues to them.

There should be reduction in the growth and influence of vested interests in all spheres of activity. While inequalities in opportunity have to be reduced, opportunities have to be created for the poor. Heavily populated urban areas should be de- congested with adequate infrastructure built in the peripheral areas. Decongestion of heavily congested urban areas will promote the development of the rural areas. This will definitely benefit the poor.

5. To conserve all available resources.

Resources pose the critical problem. While their availability can be increased through inflow of foreign assistance, internal resources have to be conserved. These resources are within the sphere of influence and control of the government. It is only the competence of the administration and the motivation the government provides to the business community that can ensure better utilization. Wasting available resources and asking for foreign assistance is like allowing a thief to enter a house knowingly and then asking the neighbor to compensate the loss.

Conservation of existing resources and ensuring the best use creates a sense of economy all over. Foreign governments develop confidence in the country's administration and competence to manage its own resources. It paves the way for the inflow of foreign capital, technical know-how and technology. The production pattern in the country needs reorganization restricting availability and pruning of luxury items.

Serious efforts are needed to locate, develop and utilize talent for achieving the best results. Efforts to prevent leakages of resources through waste, corruption, breakdown of law and order, inflation are required. Development of physical and human resources is a necessity. Enterprise in all fields of human endeavor offering prospects of wider benefits to the community deserves encouragement and reward.

6. To increase the quantum and quality of resources

Existing resources within a country are limited and their supply cannot be increased considerably all in a sudden. Demands on them are many and varied. So we have to encourage the flow of external assistance into the country. The low per capita income and the miserable conditions of living for millions of people necessitate substantial volume of foreign aid.

While conservation of resources can augment internal supply to some extent, external assistance must be available in large quantities. The advantage of having external assistance is that the benefits of scientific and technological progress in foreign countries are accessible and available for domestic use. This helps to increase the productivity of country's resources.

Attempts to increase the availability and quantum of internal resources without external assistance contain the danger of generating inflationary pressures. Conditions should be created for the inflow of capital, technology and economic assistance from all friendly countries and from international financial institutions. The existing incentives should continue.

7. To motivate all sections of the population to organize anti-poverty programmes and make them successful.

This requires conditions for greater productive employment thereby increasing the inflow of income for individuals. Efforts are necessary to de-link organizations from negative political leadership. Allegation mongering by leaders, used as an instrument for perpetuating one's interest, must be given up. It will be advantageous if power vested in the government, institutions, opposition and lying dormant in the masses, is utilized primarily for anti- poverty efforts.

Violence needs to be eschewed particularly in areas of activity thwarting attainment of anti-poverty objectives. Firmness is required in the maintenance of law and order. Encouraging voluntary distribution of wealth and community welfare activities will go a long way in attaining anti-poverty objectives. Awareness that privileged classes do have a positive role to play in the anti-poverty effort has to be created among the affluent and necessary motivation provided to them.

The national objectives have to be translated into action by leaders who have a sway over the masses. Leaders influence the minds of thousands of followers. Right and high quality leadership is undoubtedly the most important of all human resources. Talented leaders are men of vision, who make things happen, exhibit dynamism, anticipate problems and solve them before they become crises. Their task is to interpret the national goals to their followers. In all their actions leaders must have the framework of objectives illustrated earlier. They must constantly strive to persuade followers to attain them, if necessary by effecting a change of attitudes and living by example.

Leaders consist of persons in power and those in the opposition. The former must concentrate on initiating proposals consistent with the objectives. The opposition must examine the merits and worth of such proposals critically and support them after convincing that these are in the national interest. A clear grasp of anti poverty objectives will help to develop a positive approach in solving problems. Actions will yield fruitful results only if those on whom responsibility for leadership will fall later, also work towards promoting the cause of prosperity.

The problem of poverty is of great magnitude. Citizens have to be guided to play their role effectively. This can be done if they also frame objectives. This will provide the link between their efforts and those of the leaders, thereby making the task of the latter easy and successful. These objectives create awareness of the need for their contribution in certain essential areas of economic activity as members of society.

Some of the major objectives for citizens are explained below.

1. To limit family size to sustainable levels considering national interest

Needs are growing while resource are scarce. Yields from agricultural lands cannot be increased indefinitely due to the operation of the law of diminishing returns. The per capita income, which is already low, should not be allowed to decline. Land for housing is also becoming costly and its availability is limited. It is necessary to improve the standard of living of the masses.

With all these considerations it becomes necessary to restrain population growth. It is the social obligation of every citizen in our country to limit the size of the family through methods suitable to him. Realization of this objective will bring far reaching benefits to the nation. Standard of living and employment opportunities will increase. The best care, attention and education can be given to children. Law and order problems will be less and there will be a better sense of security for all citizens.

2. To regulate needs

While needs have the tendency to grow fast resources do not grow at the same pace. Limitations imposed by reduced availability of resources force one to curtail needs or modify ways of living to avoid financial disaster. The inherent difficulty in balancing growing needs and resources and the relative inelasticity of the latter must be recognized. Action is necessary to regulate certain needs and to prevent rapid growth of many others. Such a process will ease the pressure on resources of the nation.

3. To realize opportunities for self-employment

Government cannot provide direct employment to all citizens. There are limitations of resources and operational difficulties in organising massive programmes of employment generation. So the individual has to search for opportunity and acquire skills for self - employment. Those already employed except persons in the essential services, after working for some years, must try to become entrepreneurs to create more jobs. Any salaried employment should be treated as a stepping-stone for developing skills for self- employment after a minimum gestation period. It is a healthy sign that India is now having a growing strength of middle class with entrepreneurial skills and resources for investment.

4. To eliminate wastage of resources

Wastage of resources arises from the individual's carelessness and lack of foresight. Conservation makes it possible to use them at a later date. It also helps to divert them for the needs of others. In the context of growing needs and rising population the need for minimizing wastage of resources in every sphere of activity assumes great importance.

5. To contribute one's maximum in any area of economic activity

Society grows out of contributions made by individuals and institutions. Behind every institution there is an individual or a group of dedicated men responsible for its achievements. They motivate many others to make significant contributions to society. The availability and presence of many individuals with such an approach is a sure sign of progress. Some persons never expect anything in return for their work. While it is difficult to find many such men loaded with a missionary zeal for service, every individual has the potential to do something significant for society. This has to be identified, tapped, encouraged and developed.

To choose an area for contribution one has to consider the urgent needs of the nation as a whole and see how one fits into the framework. All professions seek to fulfill the national needs and goals in some way or other. The area of action for any individual is vast. To prevent frittering away of energies it is better if one chooses a specific field of activity. One must acquire adequate knowledge in that field and strive for improvements which will benefit society. This requires reforming the education system to impart practical orientation to the syllabus.

Once a field is chosen it is easy to find those who have worked in similar or allied fields and to learn from their experience. Such choice can also result in complementing the efforts of others to attain a greater degree of perfection. The field should be chosen according to the aptitude of the individual. If there is no aptitude, interest in a line of activity has to be cultivated. It is worth the effort for in the long run it pays rich dividends to the individual and to the nation.

6. To work hard with faith and discipline

Discipline is the orderly conduct of oneself by exercising restraint and channelizing energies towards desirable objectives. It is basic to the formation of character, which is vital for individual and national progress. Discipline develops one's ability and helps to avoid strife. Law and order problems are often the result of absence of such disciplined behavior. Any nation that has attained rapid and lasting progress has done it only through discipline and hard work.

Shortcuts to success are not enduring. The individual has to devote considerable effort and strain himself to attain a high degree of discipline. Faith in oneself forms the basis of confidence, which is essential for any achievement. It anchors one to the basic aptitudes discovered within oneself and propels one to action.

7. To work for the best results per period of time

Time is a critical resource. The experience during a period of time definitely leaves a result depending on the soundness of action taken during that period. To ensure that subsequent periods bring desirable, tangible and beneficial results, like any other resource, the time available should be intelligently used. Economic planning lags behind because the seriousness of time limits for implementation of programmes is not realized. Setting time limits helps one to bring out the best in oneself for the results have to be attained by a definite date. The individual is motivated to work at his maximum capacity and he tries to adopt the best available methods to execute the task.

8. To promote the absorption of technology

The world is witnessing tremendous advances in science and technology. This can considerably help to meet modern requirements of mass production and to realize economies of scale. Even though economic conditions in developing countries need labour intensive Programmes, one can ignore the importance of technology only at the risk of being bypassed by other nations. The import and adoption of technology must be considered in the context of national objectives. Every citizen has to prepare himself for the ready absorption of advanced technology from all over the world.

Knowledge has no frontiers. The key to success lies in using knowledge for attaining desirable objectives. So unless we keep abreast of the latest developments in various fields, progress becomes impossible. Side effects or unemployment have to be eliminated and counter measures devised. Absorption of technology helps to reduce inflationary tendencies in the economy and to improve the competitive position of the country in the international market.

9. To organize for good causes

The success of any society largely depends on the manner in which members organize their efforts. Without organization energy goes waste and individuals lose direction and purpose. Millions of men are without the basic necessities of life. Some one has to take over the responsibility of providing them with these. The State suffers from many limitations to improve their lot rapidly.

Hence those who have means must act. Many problems arise due to absence of right organization. The gap in essential functions results in serious losses to society and creates law and order problems. Energies of citizens must be canalized for collective benefit and various constructive ways have to be devised.

10. To contribute to social welfare measures

Citizens have to be clear about what constitutes social welfare and then do what lies within their resources and capability to attain it. Such contribution may be in the form of funds, labour, or some other useful service. People, particularly the rich, must constantly look for opportunities to serve the poor. With the growing complexity of problems individuals cannot afford to ignore the forces operating in society if they have to avoid being swept away by the currents generated by general discontent.

11. To promote a healthy neighborhood

Happiness of the individuals is considerably influenced by the relations and attitudes of neighbors. A favorable attitude helps programmes like slum clearance and other community activities. It becomes possible to undertake them with the least interruption and difficulty and to keep the vicinity hygienic and tidy. The interrelationship of individual goals of citizens in a closely situated area is easily understood. This promotes harmony and peace.

The area of conflict narrows down and some machinery for resolving differences evolves. Children also come to know the benefits of such goals and they develop a cooperative attitude towards other inhabitants of the locality. It provides a good training ground for them to learn some fundamental concepts like cooperation, which are vital for the survival and progress of the community.

12. To settle differences peacefully

Most conflicts arise from the inability of individuals to settle differences peacefully. Thus the creative energies of people are diverted towards destructive ends resulting in considerable loss of resources and output. On such occasions the machinery enforcing law and order is put to severe strain in restoring the status quo. It also becomes impossible to make improvements in areas of useful activity since the required attitude does not exist.

Much of this can be avoided if the individual develops the attitude of adopting peaceful means to resolve conflicts.

This will reduce the violence potential of situations and offer relief to the agencies enforcing law and order. They can concentrate on more important and productive areas of activity.

13. To hold on to basic values of society

Man cherishes values because they promote understanding and respect for others. Values help men to be worthy citizens of a country and to raise its prestige in the international field. Neglect of values thwarts attempts at character formation. Many ills of a country arise from the lack of awareness of the factors which constitute its strength. Basically these are character, respect for truth, tolerance towards others and active resistance to evil. Such consciousness of the country's strength backed by discipline and hard work brings success.

Part of one's time must be devoted to knowing the significance of the heritage and strength of one's country. Such an approach provides a strong base for a safe and healthy take off towards achievement of other objectives. Our duty is not only to the present generation. We inherited many good things from our ancestors. So one has to preserve the best values of this generation and pass them on to posterity. This requires consolidation of benefits, drawing lessons from the past and molding them with reference to future needs.

14. To evaluate leaders objectively

In a democracy leaders are elected by different sections of the population. Critical evaluation of the qualities and performance of leaders, though difficult in the context of a vast illiterate population, has to be attempted. Those who are educated and well informed must attempt to evaluate leaders in terms of competence and performance. The framework of national objectives will be helpful to the individual for comparing and judging the perspective of the leader. The citizen can evaluate whether actions of the leader are really conducive to the achievement of anti poverty results.

15. To work for the realization of national objectives

Actions of individuals have to be linked to national objectives. Otherwise, conflicts of interests arise, threatening their attainment. These objectives provide the framework within which the individual objectives are to be set. For instance, we desire prosperity. But without productivity the national objective of increased wealth will not be attained and ultimately all citizens will suffer.

Achievement in any field requires a starting point for action. Objectives provide such starting points in vital areas of economic activity. They provide direction. They help to measure the performance of anti poverty measures and to locate areas needing corrective action. The general objectives illustrated earlier are for minimizing conflicts in society so that vast resources now wasted, could be made available for anti poverty programmes.

Specific objectives with anti poverty orientation for each group of citizens, though not explained here, are also necessary. Individual and professional objectives will help the task of leadership, and all the three will interact and help the attainment of anti poverty objectives. While the national objectives are the concern of all citizens, the primary responsibility for their attainment devolves on the leadership.

We must have a system combining competence, ethics and values. Incompetence should not be allowed to over shadow such a system. One of the most pressing problems we face is the proliferation of incompetence in every sphere of activity. Incompetence gains momentum and asserts its supremacy. While an organization can carry on without damage with one parasite or incompetent for ten intelligent persons, it is catastrophic to have the reverse ratio. A soft democracy shelters incompetence more than any other form of government. This is because of its capacity to tolerate incompetence in the name of accommodating mediocrity and allowing representation for various splinter groups.

People form the power base in a democracy. Pressure of political parties during elections determines the choice of candidates, the voting strategy and their success. The objective is to win at any cost but not necessarily on merit and with dignity. If any one tries to do so he is generally doomed.

The incompetence of the executive to take right and timely decisions pushes citizens towards litigation. Judiciary again is slow in delivering judgment on cases. Citizens lose faith in the government. Sometimes they can't expect the final verdict even in the days of their grandchildren.

Solution lies not in adding to the number of judges but by improving the system for trial, processing of cases and reducing the number of cases coming to the judiciary. There is need for an effective mechanism to screen and weed out cases, so that they do not come before the judiciary causing waste of time.

Leadership lags behind in tapping opportunities for growth and service. The result is that the economy limps. When leadership lacks dynamism incompetence flourishes. Obsolete means of handling situations prevail. Values are thrown overboard and sane advice dries up for want of encouragement. Enthusiasm of talented individuals is dampened by the propaganda of the incompetent infernos.

Incompetence is not the monopoly of any particular section of the government. The executive, judiciary legislature all have their due share. There appears to be a silent competition in stupidity, unknowingly promoted by unrealistic approach to real life problems. Each reinforces the other and the cumulative impact is that the economy stagnates and the nation becomes weak. Talented individuals become non-entities because of their inability to seize opportunities for development and advancement.

The three wings of the government should graft inputs from value systems. This is the basis for character formation. The meaning of secularism is not correctly understood by most leaders. The most secular man was Swami Vivekananda. Can anyone say he was not concerned with humanity? Can any one say he was a votary of caste or any religion? No one will say he had no concern for the poor. He advocated universal brotherhood. Our leaders have to learn the concept of secularism from great leaders like Swami Vivekananda and Mahatma Gandhi and not from those who have half baked knowledge of spirituality and secularism. Unfortunately the inputs are not made available to those who badly need them to refine their performance.

Knowledge industry is expanding. If incompetence does not decline in inverse proportion to rise in knowledge, proliferation will take place. Many leaders will become eligible to enter the Liabilities side of the balance sheet of the nation. Their names will find place in the balance sheet of various political parties. The remedy lies in identifying the *core competence* needed in various areas like the executive, legislature and judiciary. They should be provided exposure to acquire, absorb and assimilate the skills needed to lift the economy and the country to greater heights of achievement and glory.

In a democratic framework the government is the source of leadership, and the manifestation of such leadership is through the use of power. So the task of leadership becomes one of 'power management'. Effective 'power management' is critical for fulfilling anti poverty objectives. The task of elimination of poverty is of great magnitude and it cannot be fully entrusted to private enterprise. The latter is not ripe, large and strong enough to launch a frontal attack on the problem. So we have to strengthen our power management skills.

4. Power Management

The government necessarily has to take the initiative in tackling problems of great social magnitude having far reaching implications. Economic planning becomes necessary. Such planning by the State implies concentration of power, and this power is the offspring of the political system. It is exercised through governmental leadership. So the task of the government becomes one of 'power management',

Having set objectives to benefit the people the nation's resources have to be deployed effectively. Technological advances do help to meet the growing demands of the population. But it is very difficult to increase the quantum of resources in the short term.   So apart from conserving resources it is necessary to increase productivity.

A serious threat to productivity is unproductive employment. This arises from the pressures exerted by leaders, trade unions, and the unemployed for jobs. The economy needs productivity. Businessmen who work to attain this objective need support to lay off unproductive personnel. Necessary conditions for attaining this objective must be provided by the government. Under such conditions modernization programmes have greater chance of success and there will be less resistance to change. The reduced labour strength is less likely to pose threats to the organization. It will be engaged in productive tasks, which are remunerative and satisfying. Organizations where such retrenchment takes place provide for social security benefits. They launch measures for higher productivity and efficiency. Those receiving such benefits can later take up jobs in the same organization or outside, in which case the benefits are discontinued. The retrenched personnel could be encouraged to become entrepreneurs. As an incentive the government will frame policies of financial assistance to them for starting small and medium enterprises. They can continue to get the benefits of social security for one year. This step has to be implemented boldly to relieve the pressure on jobs and to encourage self-employment.

Reward and performance must be matched and some objective criteria evolved for measuring them. Productivity research must be a compulsory feature in all areas of activity, especially in agriculture, education, health and law and order. This should aim at better community benefits. Prompt action by a few police men by way of deterrent action injuring or killing a single miscreant is preferable to the deployment of a large force achieving nothing and causing loss of several innocent lives later demoralizing the police force.

Democracy calls for people's participation. This will be freely forthcoming only if the masses are *motivated* to achieve something worthwhile. In making the individual more productive the most powerful agent is the force of motivation. It is here leadership can play an important role. When motivation - the force propelling an individual to excel his performance- is present and added to the factors of production economic progress is rapid and substantial. The task of institutions and organizations must be to motivate the human beings of concern to them. The reservoir of talent, which can motivate the masses into action, must be tapped along with other resources like land, labour, capital and enterprise.

Due to growing complexity of industrial organizations and the rising expectations of masses the limitations of material resources are felt. Resources management has become a complex activity. The two people oriented resources; labour and enterprise, have assumed importance and the quality of these two along with other factors of production determine the rate of economic growth. The most important resource required is enterprise- the ability to take calculated risks for creating wealth in the country. This talent, which is scarce, has to be developed and multiplied. Enterprising men are few and the labour force is large. There is generally a clash of interest between them. This results in wastage of precious and scarce resources. This loss can be minimized by the actions of the government. The latter has to give up the implicit policy of looking helplessly forcing the former to abdicate their right to manage industry. The condition will worsen if policies, like non-interference in labour disputes, are not discarded.

It is necessary to evaluate the employment potential of existing programmes. To encourage employment and enterprise it is worth considering tax incentives based on employment. The government's labour polices framed with the intention of setting up an egalitarian society should not have the effect of freezing enterprise.

Leadership can succeed only when it utilizes the reservoir of motivation. Fortunately India has a glorious heritage where spirituality acts as a motivating force. In the past this helped considerably to develop supra ordinary goals and made people achievement oriented. Great national leaders like Mahatma Gandhi belonged to that category.

It is essential that *motivational economics* gains importance. The core of this theory lies in utilizing governmental power and spirituality as motivating tools. Apart from propelling the masses to achieve excellence they also help to curtail unnecessary low priority needs thereby relieving pressure on resources.

This is the new economics for economic development particularly for poverty alleviation. It is doubtful whether investment alone can bring prosperity. Employment alone is not indicative of the level of prosperity. This becomes explicit when we see the prevalence of a large force of unproductive labour in different categories in many organizations. Neither investment nor employment can provide the lever to alleviate poverty. Motivation, which deserves serious consideration as a prime resource, will provide the strength to alleviate poverty.

The role of the State will be to generate opportunities so that individuals and institutions are motivated to seize and realize them, thereby increasing employment and output. The State will concentrate only on those areas directly required to be under its control for strategic reasons. It will enter other areas of economic activity only when individuals and institutions do not have the strength, competence and resources to undertake such ventures. Even here, it will try to pass on the ownership and management of such activities to private organizations gradually. This will lighten the burden of the State and save and spare its resources for more important and worthwhile projects.

Undoubtedly the leadership of a country at various levels with the help of the machinery at its disposal is responsible for achieving economic progress. In a country with socialistic goals the government bestows on itself immense powers. Here it will be of use and interest to consider the concept of power along with its implications. Power is the invisible feature that makes it obligatory on citizens or agencies in administration, to act as per the dictates of the Executive in the *national interest*. It helps to improve the *quality of life* in the country.

Leadership within the government wields considerable power, which has great potential for good or bad. Power is the essential attribute of a government. It has to be used for achieving economic progress. Thus the function of the government becomes one of effective 'power management'.

The administrative system with its various hierarchies represents the power network controlling the source and flow of power required by the thousands of 'power centers'. These 'power centers' are manned by officials for translating into action the objectives of a welfare state. Power is also derived from outside the official power structure. Various individuals and sections of people have power lying dormant in them and this can be tapped with advantage. For the individual official at the 'power centre' his competence, skill, knowledge of the situation, its obstacle potential, ability to assess the strength of the interferences, and strategies to develop and conserve power, are all decisive factors in effective power utilization. In addition there are two important assets, which considerably help to develop power and to prevent 'power erosion'. These are *discipline* and *motivation* at all levels in the power hierarchy.

The power mechanism of the government has three wings. They are the Executive, Legislature and the Judiciary. The actions of these elements have a definite impact on the degree of success for economic development. Primarily the test for successful 'power management' will be whether the actions of these three have helped to increase productivity, the income flow of the economically weaker sections, to motivate people to work towards achieving social and economic justice and to strengthen the value systems conducive to economic growth.

Apart from these objectives the following principles will have to be observed by all agencies and leaders concerned.

i. 'Power centers' will be motivated to excel in their performance and contribute to national prosperity
ii. 'Power centers' will increase their competence on a regular basis

iii. All sections of society will be motivated to excel their performance in the national interest

iv. Law and order will be maintained at any cost

v. Power will be used as a tool for motivating all sections of the community

vi. Power will be used to curb activities of harmful consequences to the community

vii. Power will be used to get the best results from the community's resources

viii. Power will be used to promote activities of positive benefits to the community

ix. Privileged sections of society will have a specific role in ensuring social and economic justice

x. Productivity will be encouraged

Some of the supporting objectives required are:

i. To use the tax system as a motivating tool for economic justice

ii. To define the role of the State as that to create opportunities for advancement of its citizens

iii. To give priority to the welfare of the unorganised masses will receive priority

iv. To avoid overlapping of functions and responsibilities of 'power centers'

v. To determine the nature of legislative and judicial support required

vi. To determine the power channel and structure appropriate to discharging the government's functions

vii. To determine the power mix i.e., written, discretionary, legal cover, enactments etc.

viii. To increase competence of persons holding various 'power centers' and of those directly under the charge of each 'power centre'.

ix.   To locate obstacles and constraints in the exercise of power and to remove them

x.   To locate power leakages and to plug them

xi.   To look for source of power within and outside the power hierarchy and to make effective use of it discreetly for achieving power objectives

xii.   To strengthen weak points

xiii.   To take the initiative for solving a problem by taking orders from the situation

xiv.   To recognize values are vital for progress.

xv.   To remember violence in any form will be put down

xvi.   To review the power needs of the various 'power centers' at regular intervals and take corrective action promptly

The task of the government does not merely stop with deploying its power to get the best results from its resources. It has to recognize that the Opposition has enormous power because of its hold on the masses. Like the various 'power centers' with power vested in them, the leadership at various levels constituting the Opposition has colossal power concealed in it. As long as the government in power taps this strength of the Opposition and diverts its energies for economic growth chances of such programmes becoming successful are greater. Such an approach becomes impossible if the Opposition does not share the responsibility. This is more so if there are numerous opposition parties who are keen not to have any unanimity of approach except to topple down the government. Stalling parliamentary proceedings non stop for over three weeks is not a healthy way of promoting economic progress.

The success of 'power management' depends on how effectively the power mechanism functions and how swiftly the various elements in the process work to conserve, develop, and build up power for attaining national objectives. Any lapse at any stage can work havoc on the power mechanism and cause break down of law and order. Deterioration in law and order weakens the power mechanism and makes it more ineffective thus thwarting progress.

Power structures constantly face challenges from within and without. There is need to identify the challenges, realize their implications and to deploy the power mechanism for corrective action. Orders have to be dictated by the situation and not by the individuals. The hierarchy is only to view the situation in its proper perspective and to issue commands when absolutely necessary. Inadequacies in 'power centers' should be met by transferring power to those points. Agitations threaten the power structure. Any delay in action paralyses it in such a manner that the agitators usurp power by sheer force of numbers and force the official 'power centre' to concede their demands.

Interference and pressure from within the power hierarchy, wrong policies, procedures, inadequate support from within, vested interests, and incompetence disrupt the power structure. The party system in a democracy has a built in bias towards enlarging the sphere and content of conflict. There exist pockets of incompetence and compartmental decision making. The danger exists that these may multiply and increase in scope and intensity as long as their existing impact on the power structure is not assessed. Political and emotional pressure poses additional threats. They set in motion various demoralizing forces, which in turn affect the power mechanism and its strength.

Corruption further weakens the power structure by forcing shift in power in favour of those who are corrupt. This builds up a zone of vested interests and camp followers demanding more time, energy, and human resources of the power system for negative results. Half-hearted exercise of power weakens the system. Break down of law and order and resulting power losses bring about a shift of power to areas which are detrimental to the national interest. This causes imbalance and further erosion of power.

The absence of a common set of well understood objectives brings about a change in the direction and flow of power. Decision-making is only a process of altering the power flow. The task of the government is only that of managing the elements in the power structure. This is one step farther from that of managing men. The process is a continuous one. Any break in the process intentional or otherwise, necessitates additional set up and start up time merely to regain lost ground.

If government experiments with this scheme of power objectives it will not only act boldly but will achieve rapid economic growth. To be effective its power should be free from adulteration and leakage. The protective sheaths of *faith, discipline and hard work* can enhance its effectiveness. This is the formula for success. The function of the government is to tap other resources through the use of power. Power objectives have to be related to other objectives of economic growth. If higher levels of leadership assume that only the lower levels have to bear the responsibility for 'power management' failure is a certainty.

Power is a distinct asset of the government. It is to be used as a resource and not as something emotionally attached to and derived from the electorate. It is not a status symbol. The roots of power lie with the people. The quality of power and its right application decisively determine the quality of life of the people. Elected politicians provide leadership in government. They provide the link between the people and the Executive. Unless these men take positive and dynamic action they will remain as leaders who follow. They must fully equip themselves to discharge their responsibilities by directing the power mechanism. The day they become real leaders motivating followers we shall have 'power management' for economic growth. This calls for development leadership.

5. Development Leadership

The basic problem facing a poor country is the inability of leadership to launch fruitful programmes and to carry the masses along with them. Although rare cases of efficiency at top levels of leadership do exist, they are inadequate to meet the challenges and magnitude of the problems. Leadership, which walks on stilts, cannot make significant progress towards poverty abolition.

Actions of leaders both in power and in the opposition have contributed towards inflating the needs of the people and depleting the nation's resources. Any programme of leadership development must achieve the basic requirements of the people with reference to these two arms of poverty i.e. needs and resources. The purpose here is not to discuss the techniques of developing leadership. Our focus of attention is only on what is immediately needed for abolition of poverty. The span of vision required by leaders can thus be narrowed down to two areas. These are:

1. To reduce the needs of the affluent population to basic necessities, essential articles and services and to conserve resources.

2.   To devise and develop various techniques suited to local conditions and implement them to attain results in the area of poverty abolition.

Three elements are hostile to the realization of these objectives. One is the increasing *materialistic attitude* of the people fanned by desires to imitate the affluent sections of society. Another is the *disrespect for law and order* displayed by many sections of population including many levels of leadership. The third element is *corruption* by men in responsible positions. While the first one inflates the needs of individuals and thus distorts the demand, the second and third cause huge erosion of resources. According to a research report by Global Financial Integrity, India lost Rs 9.6 lakh crores in illicit outflows during 1948 to 2008 on account of corruption, bribery and kickbacks, criminal activities and efforts to shelter wealth from the country's tax authorities. Present value of this leakage of resources comes to Rs.21 lakh crores. Thus India lost Rs 72000 crores annually. This amount could wipe out India's external debt as of 2008 and leave Rs.10.5 *lakh crores* for poverty alleviation. Thus there is pressing the need for plugging leakages through corruption.

Widespread destruction of property and productive resources during a countrywide agitation results in loss amounting to crores of rupees. It is easy to destroy wealth, property and resources of such a magnitude in a few days. But it takes several months' effort, financial and technical assistance, for reconstruction of lost facilities and many years to recoup the loss completely. In the context of the state undertaking the responsibility for major economic activity, even a modest rate of five percent 'corruption allowance' depletes the resources considerably.

The three enemies of poverty referred to earlier, demand qualities of leadership deeply rooted in values and supported by our cultural heritage. Such qualities include austerity, non-violence and integrity. Austerity helps to curtail non priority needs. An attitude of non-violence enables one to seek solutions through ways other than loss of productive resources. Integrity enables one to withstand corruptive influences. These three qualities, which constitute the antidote to poverty, are crystallized in the concept of *character*.

Though they are needed in all citizens, these qualities are essential for leaders. Without them leadership will never be able to lead and inspire the masses. Such a leadership will be non-performing. Any programme of leadership development must stress the need and methods for development of these qualities. Basic *values* have to be culled out, codified and imbibed. Only a leadership deeply rooted in such values and living by example can have great impact on the followers. The masses are inspired to emulate their example. Under such conditions corruptive influences lose their hold and there is greater conservation and productive use of resources.

A comprehensive leadership development programme has to be evolved. This requires *training* of leaders and those individuals with potential. The objective of the training programme should be:

• To train leaders at different levels of activity
• To provide essential background required for a national perspective and
• To develop skills in solving problems.

The training is solely for developing leadership to achieve economic growth on right lines. The different levels determined geographically are only classifications for administrative convenience. Objectives could be achieved through a training programme spread over a period of four years. The duration could be varied according to the level of leadership.

The programme can include the following subjects:

• Character and economic development
• Constitution
• Cultural and religious forces
• Decision-making
• Environment of the country

98

- Factors promoting economic development
- Factors retarding economic growth
- Fiscal policy and banking policy
- International economic situation
- Management of resources
- Monetary system and economic growth
- Motivation and productivity
- National objectives/policies/strategies
- Planning and implementation
- Prices, productivity and output
- Problems in administration
- Quantitative techniques in decision-making
- Science and economic growth

The programme can richly draw from the experience of various developing countries, which have successfully managed their economies. Contemporary economic events could be chosen for analysis. Emphasis will be on saving cost, time and effort in attaining results. Continuous research will be necessary to revise the syllabus to reflect the latest experience and problems of such countries. It could be a four tier programme involving different but related levels of leadership. Economic development is not merely the result of financial and technical assistance. It has to be achieved through effective management of society through quality leadership.

The training and development proposed should be based on observations of problems of sick as well as growing economies and their solutions. Protests and demonstrations cannot attain objectives. As Prof. Samuelson has observed, "slogans of socialism or banners, and constitutions are not sufficient to promote rapid industrial progress."

The national government is primarily responsible for economic development. But advanced countries could devise productive ways of economic assistance e.g., a package for creation of infrastructure facilities in a specific territory consisting of a group of villages. These are elementary education, secondary education, health, social security, energy, water, transport, power, roads, railways, ports, transportation systems and effective service delivery

Initially this could be implemented on an experimental basis. The current thinking in business points to greater awareness of the Corporate Social Responsibility. Tie up with large corporate business houses will provide social entrepreneurship, professional inputs and resources to achieve the objective of poverty reduction. Such assistance will keep in view the objective of generating leadership all over the territory.

The core of the programmes will be to stress the need for developing an attitude that will reflect that:

- A sense of urgency and regard for time is essential for progress.
- Breakdown of law and order destroys resources
- Corruption accentuates poverty.
- Employment is meaningful only if it is productive.

- Improvement in the quality of life of citizens is the concern of leadership
- Motivation and productivity are essential for removing poverty
- Production is as important as distribution.
- Promoting the welfare of the unorganised masses and those below the poverty level deserves top priority
- Taxation is to be used as a motivating tool
- The role of the State is to create opportunities for advancement of citizens *and*
- Values are important for progress

Leadership development in the long run has to come from a change in education policy. This should concentrate on changing the attitudes of citizens for the better. It should focus on creating attitudes that will achieve efficiency, diligence, orderliness, punctuality, frugality, honesty, rationality, Integrity and self-reliance. It should also create in them preparedness for change and alertness to opportunities. Many who really take education seriously find the tentacles of misery and demotivation coiling on them. They seize the earliest opportunity to seek jobs outside the country. Advanced countries provide assistance and training to persons in poor countries. Ultimately they benefit by having the services of trained persons who end up in serving them.

If a breakthrough is to be made for a solution to the problem of poverty, it is essential that this trend be reversed. Research activity in educational institutions must concentrate on the areas of motivation, values and economic progress. Undoubtedly importance has to be given to character development. The relationship between character and economic development should be recognized and programmes designed to form a practical course module in this area. In addition areas chosen should include improvement of law and order and elimination of corruption. This calls for an institutional approach.

Thus the key instrument for abolition of poverty is development leadership. Quality leadership reinforced by a well-educated population sharpens it. It strengthens national and individual character through setting examples. The benefits of education, though slow and time consuming, will be steady and lasting. Quality leadership and sound education interact. Character formation has a multiplier effect. It also accelerates capital formation by assisting conservation of resources and thus promotes economic growth and abolition of poverty.

It is relevant here to remember the following words of Swami Vivekananda. "So long as the millions live in hunger and ignorance, I hold every person a traitor who, having been educated at their expense pays not the least heed to them".

In the task of poverty abolition, the rich have a positive role. Many among them have been pace setters. They enjoy high standards of living, which imply a varied and more complex hierarchy of needs. As mentioned earlier one arm of poverty is the growing need hierarchy. The rich are achieving higher levels of living and the poor are unable to maintain even their existing levels. In this context the view expressed by the famous economist and Nobel Laureate Jan Tin Bergen is of great significance.

:"Generally the rich of the earth should prepare themselves for a simpler life in the future. The leading philosophy of the present, which always asks for more material goods and does not attach much value at simplicity of life or modesty in claims, has to be replaced by alternative philosophies, and surely much could be learned from Mahatma Gandhi's words and example. The real values of life do contain sufficient quantity of food and shelter; but it is not necessary to have the luxuries now aimed at. Cultural values will have to be upgraded again."

This view of the Nobel Laureate deserves serious consideration by all agencies, national and international, concerned with poverty abolition. If there is one thing certain and is badly needed, it is the development and cultivation of a value system which alone can impart strength and stability to any solution. Great leaders have shown the way. We have to follow them and look for areas for further improvement. Then only we can remove poverty from the face of this planet.

6. Motivational Economics

Having set anti-poverty objectives the nation's resources of land, labour, capital and enterprise have to be utilized effectively. Democracy calls for people's participation. The most essential resource required is enterprise, i.e. the ability to take calculated risks for creating wealth. This talent has to be developed and augmented. Leadership can succeed only if it utilizes the reservoir of motivation in individuals whom it leads. This takes us to the need for a new economics for poverty alleviation. That is Motivational Economics.

The role of the State will be to generate opportunities so that individuals and institutions are motivated to seize and realize them, thereby increasing employment and output. Undoubtedly the leadership at various levels with the help of the administrative machinery at its disposal is responsible for achieving economic progress. Let us hope it will rise to the occasion to lift the unfortunate millions from the morass of poverty.

Economics is concerned with production and distribution of goods and services ensuring equitable distribution and promoting the welfare of all people. The importance of the subject is realized by all countries and international financing and development agencies. The greatness of the subject in promoting human welfare is recognized and

Nobel Prize has been instituted in the last half century. Yet there is dissatisfaction among economists, administrators and sections of people over the ineffective manner in which resources are utilized. They are concerned about the prevalence of pockets of poverty with wide disparity in income distribution.

We have come a long way from the days of Adam Smith, passing through the days of Keynesian economics and drawing richly from Welfare economics. But theories and techniques prove to be inadequate to meet the epic challenge of the modern world of rising expectations and complex problems. A solution cannot be considered satisfactory merely in terms of increasing production and national wealth. The most effective means of distribution and that to tackle poverty has to be designed.

Though the importance of the human resource has gained recognition, it has not been utilized to its maximum potential. Refinements of this resource have been taken up in detail under the categories of entrepreneurship and leadership. But even here we are stuck when it comes to poverty alleviation and income distribution. It forces us to think in terms of further refinements in the use of resources and to discover untapped sources.

It is here a penetrating intellect finds a lead towards solution though it may not be perfect and of immediate benefit. In the absence of alternatives we have to give it a trial and make a beginning. This is the area of motivation. The human being, a critical resource, has to be motivated to excel his performance with available and other accessible tools which are least costly. This is the thrust area - *motivational economics*.

In Motivational Economics tools of economics are applied for motivating the human being, to achieve results to reduce disparities in income, to be more productive and to contribute to the growth of the gross domestic product. We shall consider briefly the framework in which this can be accomplished.

The individual is the centre of economic activity. The State is only a catalyst. It has to facilitate the individual to increase productivity and to enrich his contribution to society. For this the State lays down broad targets for increase in gross national product and for reducing disparities in income for poverty alleviation. For this without any bias or prejudice, available sources of knowledge for conservation of resources and increasing their availability with sustainability should be tapped.

Apart from the known resources the reservoir of talent within the individual together with the value system, should be utilized. The government should provide the conditions for developing this input within the individual and facilitate its blooming so that he commands other resources for attaining common objectives. There should not be any shirking of responsibility by the State for resisting and removing hurdles which stand in the way of attaining these objectives.

Our country is a soft state tolerant of wastage, looting, destruction and erosion of resources through channels of corruption and breakdown of law and order. Widespread agitations by the people and political parties should not be chosen as a way of solving problems or for meeting the objectives. This will require building *core competence* in the executive, legislature and the judiciary apart from business and industry. The emphasis will be on gaining familiarity with the problems of poverty alleviation and to imbibe unorthodox techniques of *character formation* on a par with capital formation. The earlier this is attempted the nearer we will be towards a lasting solution.

Here a few lines of explaining the need for motivation are considered relevant. The present tendency of discouraging or even penalizing law abiding citizens and those who take care of themselves with least burden to the State, should give way to motivating them to live a socially useful life and to contribute to the growth of the economy and progress of society.

In a democracy many politicians are catapulted to positions of power by some unusual combination of circumstances. They enjoy a mass base. Many of them lavishly promise to do what they cannot do and what they will not do. But their existence depends on votes. Somehow they command a following. Some of them fit in with the definition "a leader is one who follows". They blindly do what the followers ask and not what is prudent. While opposing government policies and actions they firmly believe that their duty is to oppose anything the treasury benches bring forth regardless of the merits of the case. In this process they mobilize the support of a vast multitude of people who have nothing else to do except creating nuisance of various kinds. Such nuisance includes laying road blocks, setting fire to public transport, holding demonstrations, organising long and ten -deep processions blocking the entire road, preventing even those who are in dire need of hospitalization reaching their destination and several innumerable acts of nuisance and vandalism. Ultimately public property is damaged and even private property is not spared. Pelting stones is revelry for them. This causes injuries to many. When the police arrive on the scene many of them run away and disappear. The leader is the first to escape. He believes in the escape philosophy practiced successfully by a leader who led a team of fifty to a forest. The trek was interrupted by the sudden appearance of a huge leopard, which threatened them. The great leader proclaimed (to instill confidence and courage in the followers) "Those who are afraid of the leopard fall over me". The followers faithfully obeyed. They were on top and the leader was at the bottom. The leopard pounced on them and snatched away one fellow who was on top. After it left the leader came out of his place of safety, coming-out of the clutches of all those who were above him. He shouted: Has the leopard left? I knew it would. My strategy worked." He saved himself at the cost of man on top. Such leaders and their followers have a destructive mind. They give only loss and misery to those who are law-abiding. The government grants them pardon and rewards them because their party is in power and they have the support.

In contrast a law-abiding citizen suffers all harassment. He does not cause any damage to life and property. He pays taxes. But he is put to great misery and agony because of the acts of the vandals. He does not get any incentive to continue his good conduct and behavior. Is he not entitled to get bonus for his good conduct, help in preserving law and order and in helping the government to conserve resources? This is a serious matter which motivational economics should consider in public interest.

7. Rural Development

According to World Bank reports about two-thirds of India's people depend on rural employment for a living. In 2007/08, agricultural growth touched 4.9% facilitated by a good monsoon, greater production of high-value crops, an increase in the minimum support prices for grains, and the rise in global prices for agricultural products. However, in the last two years, the agriculture sector grew at only about 2.5-3% on account of lower rainfall and the worst drought since 2002/03. Going forward, it will be essential for India to build a productive, competitive, and diversified agricultural sector and facilitate rural, non-farm entrepreneurship. Encouraging policies that promote competition in agricultural marketing will ensure that farmers receive better prices. This takes us to the need for rural development.

The level of inequality has risen high. Hunger in India has reached its highest level in decades. Rural economies across India are on the verge of collapse due to liberal policies of the government of India since the 1990s. The human cost of 'liberalization' has been great. Suicides of farmers in India during 1997 to 2007 were estimated at 200,000, according to official statistics.

Any attempt at rural development must give priority to tackle the problem of rural poverty, Unemployment is extensive. Development programmes have not left much impact in the rural areas. We shall consider the framework of action for rural development.

We can clearly isolate compact areas of 50 sq. kms each and map them in detail. Each area thus determined could be termed as *Intensive Development Centre* (IDC). A team of professionals will guide this centre. They will consist of management and productivity experts located in the regions and zones. Detailed programmes will be prepared for each centre and targets set with reference to the estimated increase in per capita income.

The IDC will be treated as a system and the various agencies providing inputs and marketing the output will be treated as sub systems. They will have well defined and well knit objectives. Initially this concept will be implemented in a few selected territories on an experimental basis. Based on the progress the scheme will be extended to other areas. Simultaneous attempts will be made to decongest urban areas creating a wave of development activity towards the villages. Thus a two-pronged attack on the problem of rural poverty is envisaged.

For implementation of the programme of rural development through IDCs, a clear demarcation of the rural areas is necessary. Though this is difficult, for our purpose, the rural area may be defined as one without any large or medium industry and which is predominantly agricultural with little basic amenities of living. It is also necessary to isolate the urban areas along with their peripheries excluding them from the sphere of rural development .A compact cluster of villages, e.g., 50 sq. kms in area, with identifiable boundaries should be mapped and all data recorded in the map. Thus will include all data relevant to development, e.g. schools, colleges, hospitals, resource based industries, service centers etc. This map is a prime necessity.

The data map should be used for the preparation of budget, i.e., statement of needs and resources of the area. The needs of the local people could be assessed in terms of total purchasing power desirable to fulfill the minimum needs. To start with, this could be determined taking into account the total number of people in the IDC area multiplied by double the per capita income. For e.g. if 10000 persons are in an IDC area total purchasing power required will be equivalent to this number multiplied by double the per capita income.

The existing average purchasing power in the area and the per capita income in the IDC could be determined and deducted from the estimated purchasing power to be generated. Based on the gap in purchasing power to be bridged, the investment will be assessed. Due to the operation of the multiplier and acceleration principles, the investment required may be less. The principle of management by exception will be applied in locating areas for investment. For e.g. if there is adequate number of schools in the area, no new school will be set up during the period under consideration.

Before setting up any other facility in the area, the extent of idle capacity, if any, in the adjacent centre will be considered. Except in the case of specialized skills, emphasis will be given to local residents for employment. Once the residents are trained or permanent hands are available, outsiders could be moved to other centers.

For development of rural Intensive Development Centers, resources could be raised in many ways. One source is the government, which makes allocations for various territories under the national plans or area development programmes. We can determine the adequacy or inadequacy of funds provided for executing the programmes. Apart from this source, public and private firms in proximity to the IDCs could be approached and motivated to provide assistance. They could finance directly some programmes or depute trained personnel in different fields to administer the programmes.

For such services the government could compute the cost and give tax exemptions. This should be considered as encouraging social responsibility of business. The inflow of remittance from outside should be considered for determining total financial assistance required for the Centre. This requires an organization to prepare plans and detailed programmes of implementation for each IDC. A proper mix of unemployed graduates and trained personnel could man these centers guided by experienced hands that will cover a cluster of ten (or a viable number) centers under their jurisdiction. IDCs of ten will form a Regional Development Centre. Coordination will be effected at each of the administrative centers (RDCs and ZDCs) with the centers in charge of urban development and other government agencies at a higher level.

Simultaneous action will be taken by the urban development department in each city to decongest territories witnessing over crowding and excessive development. This will be a continuous process. Any decongestion move will be based on study of flow of people from the rural or suburban areas to the city for such services. A study determining the extent to which the services could be dispersed will precede this. After study of the flow of people from each area to the city, schools, colleges, hospitals, government offices, etc. could be dispersed. This will also help to reduce the strain on the transportation system. Purchasing power will get diffused in the suburban areas and gradually percolate into the rural areas.

The success of the programme of IDCs needs an effective organization. At the IDC level this will be located within the IDC, as far as possible. For a group of IDCs the entire task of rural development will be considered as a total system. Objectives to ensure all round development of IDCs to attain a minimum level of per capita income will be laid down. While the IDC organization will be the primary agency to plan, implement and monitoring, the inputs and the logistics support will be provided by various agencies constituting the subsystems. These are: inputs procuring agency, public/private sector firms, and social/ voluntary organizations, private individuals/cooperatives within the IDCs, government agencies, output marketing agency, banks and post offices. The last two are concerned with mobilizing external remittances coming to the people in the IDC area. The data will be helpful to determine the availability of funds within the IDC from people's own resources.

The IDC will define the system objectives with reference to the minimum requirements of the area. This will be within the broad framework of the policy for rural development to fulfill considerations of national interest. The system objectives could be:

1. To generate average purchasing power to exceed the per capita income of the territory, and to double it in five years

2. To provide employment at least to one able bodied member from each family

3. To increase productivity of the resources in the IDC area

4. To provide or supplement the expertise available in the IDC area for attainment of objectives.

5. To provide the inputs necessary for attainment of IDC programme and

6. To set up industrial and agro processing units which will utilize local resources

Successful attainment of system objectives requires objectives for the various subsystems, which are illustrated below:

The Inputs Procuring Agency will have to determine the adequacy and extent of input availability within the IDC area, the quantum, timing and nature of input to ensure availability of such inputs and to prepare detailed input budgets.

The corporate and commercial organizations will have objectives to determine the number of IDCs that could be taken up for intensive care and assistance, the nature and assistance to be given, the type and number of experts to be provided and their duration, training needs of the IDCs and devise ways to meet them and to provide financial assistance to the IDCs.

The objectives of social and voluntary organizations will be to determine the area within the IDC where effective service could be rendered, to provide trained personnel for the task to be undertaken by the IDC, and to mobilize funds for production needs within the IDC.

Government agencies form another sub system. They will set objectives to provide all assistance and support required for IDCs, to coordinate with RDCs and ZDCs and to avoid overlapping functions. They will also determine the extent of deficit in inputs including finance and take corrective measures, It will be their responsibility to determine the impact of decongestion (de-urbanization) programmes and to locate pockets of poverty and in cooperation with the RDCs and ZDCs evolve programmes for implementation.

Commercial banks will have to recast their objectives for lending to IDCs. The present policy of micro enterprise financing will have to be extended on a large scale. Similar objectives will be necessary for other institutions concerned with financing and training of personnel for IDCs. Another subsystem, the marketing and distributing agency, will set objectives to market output generated and to ensure economic price realization.

The strategy for rural development for poverty alleviation has unique features. It does not approach the problems of rural development in isolation or piecemeal. It minimizes chances of occurrence of pockets of undeveloped areas. It is village oriented and attempts development of an intensive development centre- IDC, from within and by promoting a wave of de- urbanization. The two-pronged attack with a systems approach with various coordinated subsystems will ensure all round development, which could be accelerated or regulated as per need. It is worth implementing this idea at least in a few territories. This will help to assess the operational difficulties if any and to improve it before implementing it over a larger area. In fact, this is the strategy towards which leadership in poor countries should move, act and succeed. The Unique Identity System and information technology will help to accomplish the objectives rapidly.

8. Social Security for the Poor

The world is in the grip of the globalization phenomenon. Billionaires are increasing in thousands. At the same time there are billions of poor who cannot afford two square meals a day, let alone the necessities of civilized life. There is no social security cover for most of them.

India adopted a constitution declaring the country to be a Sovereign Democratic Republic guaranteeing to all its citizens equality of opportunity, and justice, economic and social. The real prosperity of a country is indicated by the extent of social security provided to its citizens, employment, health care, living standards, quality of life and dignity of citizens. So far social security for under privileged population on a national scale has not been thought of seriously by the governments. The fear that grips the leaders in government is that resources of huge magnitude cannot be found. It is here a change in approach to the problem and its solution is necessary. Where resources constraints exist priorities are a must. The poorest of the poor, the bottom 27% in the below poverty level section of the population have to be identified. This can be in terms of their geographical spread and basic needs.

It is tragic and an irony of fate that in a country with 27% of the population below the poverty line, compensation for rise in prices is given at regular intervals as allowances to some sections of society who are affluent .This equals the salary after a few years. It is also painful to see that every five years salaries are revised for all categories of government servants .The arrears come to a heavy amount and accrue as a windfall. This creates a situation that the government has to incur additional burden of Rs.20000 crores annually

The logic is strange indeed. If inflation justifies increasing the level of compensation for those having a decent income far above the subsistence level, nothing need be provided for those who do not have even the means of getting one meal a day. It implies seeing some men as human beings and others as human pigs. This thinking does not fit in with the values of a civilized society claiming to be progressive.

The immediate task before any democracy is not merely to get better results within the existing framework of economic and social institutions. It is to mould and recondition these institutions so that they contribute effectively to the realization of wider and deeper values. The Indian government has given stress to values by incorporating them in the Directive Principles of State Policy. These are fundamental in the governance of the country. It shall be the duty of the State to apply these principles in making laws. The State shall try to promote the welfare of the people by securing and making as effectively as it may a social order in which justice, social, economic and political, shall inform all the institutions of national life (Art.38). It shall in particular direct its policy toward securing:

i that all citizens, men and women, equally, have the right to an adequate means of livelihood

ii. that the ownership and control of the material resources of the community are so distributed as best to serve the common good;

iii. that the operation of the economic system does not result in the concentration of wealth and means of production to the common detriment (Art.39)

In pursuance of the contents of these principles it is imperative that the resources of the corporate sector, including the public sector, should be utilized for giving relief to the poor. To make a beginning, as a measure of social security for the really poor, those below the poverty line, and unemployed adults could be considered as target groups. This is the edifice on which anti poverty efforts of the future is to be built. The social security proposed is a concept which provides for a minimum regular income to poor citizens below the BPL. This includes the unemployed above 18, enabling all to ward off starvation using social security plank as the base and to strive for further progress.

Basic needs in terms of food, clothing, shelter, health and education have to be met. Taking the family as the unit and assuming an average size of five members per family the BPL section of the population will have 60 million families. 'A' category represents those at the starvation level without access to housing, clothing, health care and education. 'B' category consists of slightly better off sections, i.e., those above starvation level having some form of shelter but not other necessities.

The number and location of families under each category can be determined. For e.g., under 'A' category we may have 20 million families spread over the most economically backward states. These families are eligible for higher degree of assistance under the Social Security System (SSS). For illustration every citizen in the BPL category including unemployed individual above 18 deserves eligibility under the SSS. This classification is for administrative convenience only.

While attempting to evolve a scheme of social security we thus determine the needs of the BPL population and the resources position. In this context the corporate sector both private and public, presents a ready source. India's

GDP is estimated at to $1.09 trillion. Two percent of this comes to $21.8 billion. This amount could provide for essential needs of those below the poverty line. Taking the below poverty level population as 305 million, the per capita availability for social security cover will be $70.For ease of calculation the dollar is converted into rupees. This amount-Rs. 3150, could be allocated for various types of insurance cover for the poor. This is illustrated below:

Life insurance Rs 1000

Heath insurance Rs150

Economy housing insurance premium Rs 1000

Premium for higher education Rs 500

Public Provident Fund Rs 500

Based on the family size multiples of these amounts could be taken as the allocation per family. This is to start with and in subsequent years the percentage of contribution in relation to the GDP could be raised gradually until it reaches a desirable level providing essential needs for a healthy living. The recovery of the share of the GDP could be made from each public and private sector firm without any exception. Taking the average family size as five the benefit by insurance cover available for each family will be Rs 15750. Together with any income already available with the individual the total fund availability will increase with the added benefit of insurance cover for health, education and housing in the BPL category. BPL persons can be taken as those having an income of less than Rs. 11250 per year. This figure is prior to the various types of insurance cover proposed under the social security scheme envisaged. This could be divided into two classes- A and B.

A Rs 7500 and below

B Rs 7501-Rs 12500

For determining this classification and for identification, separate color cards could be given to them with photograph of the individual, establishing the relationship with head of the family. Weightage can be given to the BPL category which is worst hit Once a member crosses the BPL level by deriving income from any regular source of employment, his name will be removed from the eligibility list for assistance. He can continue in the various insurance schemes already initiated but will have to pay the premium from own funds and not with state support. Fresh additions to the list of unemployed will be made and such persons will become eligible for benefits under the scheme. The introduction of the Unique Identification System (UIS) will make the task easy.

Definite long term benefits accrue by way of participation in various insurance schemes. Life Insurance will bring Rs

75000 for a family of five at the end of 15 years. . Housing will be ensured. Some cash will accrue through the Public Provident Fund(PPF). Education insurance will bring at least one member in the family to get higher education which will improve employment prospects and thus bring additional income. Health insurance will look after the medical needs of the family though modestly. A house will be provided with basic amenities. The cash accrual can be used for the acquisition of a better house or as savings for the rainy day. PPF will bring Rs 11250 over 15 years. In all the accrual in 15 years will be at least Rs86250. What is provided here is only an outline and a framework which has to be worked out in detail for implementation

9. Global and National Leadership

Robert McNamara, former President of the World Bank observed in the nineteen seventies, "It is the failure of leaders in both developed and developing countries directly to address the problem of raising the quality of life that is the major cause of the fact that 800 millions of people are now in absolute poverty".

The problem of poverty dominates the discussions of all top leaders of the world. Despite the tremendous advancement of science and technology the problem remains unsolved. Various measures are evolved and implemented by governments all over the world to manage resources effectively and to realize the maximum benefits to people badly hit by the spear of poverty. Everywhere economic growth is worshipped as the most laudable objective. These efforts are supplemented by the contributions of international agencies like the World Bank and the Asian Development Bank.

In spite of all these efforts the problem of poverty poses a perennial challenge and it still raises its ugly head. The growth in national income and per capita income is rendered insignificant. The galloping inflation and growing population in many countries often neutralize it. This trend is aggravated by the scarcity of some essential goods and services.

Government is the fountainhead of power, which is manifested through policies and strategies at various levels. The role of government in a scheme of poverty eradication should be to motivate the affluent sections of society to transfer surplus resources to the poor and to provide the necessary administrative framework and infrastructure through legislative and executive action. Its important asset is power, which has to be treated as a resource and used as a lever to influence the behavior of all other resources.

In a democracy this resource of power is vested in the elected representatives of the people. It takes various forms. The Executive, Legislature and the Judiciary exercise it. These institutions have to use it in a coordinated manner for poverty eradication.

This calls for poverty abolition objectives at the global level by international agencies. This should not be confined to economic objectives only. Any area of human activity which will help to solve the problem should be considered for evolving objectives. Broadly the objectives could cover the following areas.

Conservation of resources: This can be achieved by preventing waste and leakage of resources.

Increasing productivity of resources: This can be attained by improving techniques, methods, practices.

Allocating *priorities*: This can be attained by allocating more resources to produce goods and services to meet the basic necessities of the poor people.

Sustainability of population, environment, and resources: This can be achieved by persistent efforts at educating the people.

Use of available *wisdom* handed over through ages: Here *values* have a very vital role. This is least expensive, pollution free and always has a conserving impact and influence. *Character* has a very great role in promoting economic development. This is the least expensive but most effective tool for development. It is deeply rooted in the value system and wisdom we have inherited over the ages.

The failure of democracy to make significant progress in the areas of poverty abolition is due to the failure of leadership to conserve and canalize power and to use it as catalyst for development activity that can substantially benefit the poor. Thus the problem of poverty has to be tackled in the area of leadership.

Poor countries do not have as many problem solving leaders as problem creating ones. The latter mislead the masses and their actions result in considerable wastage of resources. The answer to the question of poverty lies in the creation of a society in which such perilous deception of the unthinking masses is no longer possible. High quality leadership with the will to solve problems alone can achieve this.

10. Character and Development

Economic development is a global objective. All countries want to achieve higher rate of growth to provide citizens higher living standards, national prosperity and a higher quality of life. But have they achieved real progress?. Is growth subject to sustainability of resources of all kinds? Has character any role in economic development? We shall briefly consider these aspects and examine the need for any corrective action.

Some countries achieve economic growth at phenomenal rates. The standards of living of their citizens have gone up. At the same time many countries find their growth neutralized by the growing population. They lack access to resources and technology and are unable to command them.

However, there are limits to economic growth. The world's resources are limited and exhaustible over a period of time. So wisdom demands we use them judiciously and develop other resources which will not deplete and which can make a vital contribution to growth with sustainability. We have to identify other resources including intangibles. Just as 'time' has come to be considered as a resource needing proper and productive utilization, why not we consider character as a resource. Why not make a sincere effort to develop it among all citizens so that the whole world benefits substantially.

This has been a serious lacuna in the theory of economic development. Economists talk about labour as a resource or factor of production. But with refinement of this factor through character the results increase many fold. Though at times reference is made to character development, no concerted effort has been made by experts, particularly management and economic professionals. Except for occasional references to value systems no serious research has been done to realize their potential as a resource.

It is laudable to have several Nobel Laureates in economics. But how many have seriously examined the possibility of developing and use of character as a tool of economic development. This will occur to an intelligent mind if it has the will to accept ideas and to apply them. We need not go far to discover it. Already tested tools are available in our ancient scriptures and wisdom.

Economic planning and progress have been unsteady, with exceptions, because of the serious omission to recognize, develop and apply character as a vital input. We now recognize the human being as an important resource. We have so many human resource development programmes. We have centers of excellence. But how many centers of character development exist?. Huge wastage of resources occurs due to destructive forces and corruption. These can be prevented considerably or their impact minimized by character development.

The primary task for accomplishment of the objective of character development is mind control. This is essential before we impart any serious education. Unfortunately this is totally ignored due to misconceptions and disregard for values. We try hard to control all other resources outside man. But we do not seriously consider the value and potential of the intangible resources *within* man and to develop and control them for common good. When mind control is attained faculties are better trained and developed through education. This will imbibe qualities of faith, discipline and hard work. Together they ensure success.

Once mind control is achieved technical, human and conceptual skills can be developed rapidly, and with great benefit. It prevents conflicts and even if they occur they are resolved at the earliest stage. Presence of large number of individuals with character will not give room for conflicts. It will eliminate the tendency to be corrupt, and promote mutual help and cooperation. The incidence of criminality and unethical conduct in all areas of human activity, particularly in politics and business, will be considerably reduced. There will be less need for law enforcement and policing, less waste, better distribution of goods and services, well defined priorities, and industrial and social harmony.

It is worth setting up institutions for research and training in character development. Plenty of research material is available from ancient heritage literature and scriptures. We have to take out the principles and make case studies. They have to be made applicable to present day conditions. This is not impossible.

In the same environment men of character have performed exceedingly well without becoming a prey to temptations of any kind. Others succumb to evil influences resulting in wastage of resources. We appeal to the Nobel Laureates, governments and the rich to earmark part of their funds for character development and to pool their brains for achievement in this critical area. The examples and achievements of Japan and Korea should be studied and adopted to suit local needs and conditions.

It is important to remember and ensure that scientific advancement should match with the morality the society can hold. If there is an adverse imbalance it can only bring disastrous results. By character development on a large scale we can avoid this and reduce inequality and global harmony. Every citizen can ponder over these thoughts and do his maximum after convincing himself of the need.

We can achieve the best results from character development. Otherwise we will be creating problems and then trying to find imperfect solutions. Problems of conflict management, stress management, anger management, and probably foolishness management will continue and plague our society.

We go and grasp the root of the malady when we build character. Materialistic economic progress with the best brains cannot solve the problems of mankind and poverty unless character is developed and imparted as an ingredient. Those great souls who gave ancient wisdom made a tremendous contribution to society without expecting anything in return. They had only the welfare of mankind in view. If we do not draw on their wisdom for lasting and sustainable progress we will not succeed. This is something we can say with certainty and which is as certain as death. If we act wisely we will have a wonderful world with a band of devoted individuals dedicated to ensure a better quality of life on this planet.

Problem of sustainability of the human population has been haunting us for long. Population increases take place in economically poor countries depressing living standards. Physical resources are depleted at a faster rate due to economic development and shortages in many sectors appear. The resource crunch leaves its impact on the poor whose basic needs are not met. Poverty stares at them and instability, strife, discontent and disorder have become daily occurrences in many parts of the world.

Resources crunch badly affect those already poor. The inefficiency of the economic system results in misdirected development of the economy driven by market forces and greed and not by need and social justice. More and more resources are diverted to channels producing goods and services catering to the needs of the rich and where profit is high.

The result is that the gap between the rich and the poor is widening. This is seen glaringly after the advent of globalization. The rich command more of purchasing power and more resources of all kinds. This reduces the share of the poor. We see cases of the poor people selling lands which are cornered by the rich. The poor move to remote areas and the steep increase in land prices makes it almost impossible for them to own land and meet their housing needs. Inflation in such countries eats away the purchasing power and renders disposable income insignificant.

Poverty is a dark scar on humanity. It is a source of instability and strife. We cannot wait indefinitely for a solution to this problem. Governments all over the world must have the determination, faith and will to solve it. A time frame is a must but often it cannot be met due to pressure of circumstances. However, we must look for areas where with the available knowledge a solution is possible.

Unfortunately in the name of perverse primitive misconceptions in the name of modernity and secularism value system is neglected by leaders who owe their positions and success due to negation of value systems and wisdom. Instead many of them silently worship criminality and embezzlement. If we see the real factor behind the success of great men who have demonstrated real leadership, we will be convinced they were men of character and their actions were deeply rooted in a rich value system. They derived strength from spirituality. They served the people.

They shook the world facing challenges, overcoming them and lived a life of sacrifice. They enjoyed the happiness arising from a sense of fulfillment. World leaders have to set examples and others in the hierarchy will follow. Thousands of pages can be written on the role of character, values and spirituality in ensuring world prosperity. But what is required is an ounce of practice rather than a ton of talk.

The sooner we act the easier will be our progress towards poverty alleviation. The rich have to take the lead in renouncing the low priority areas in resource utilization. They will do well to release resources or the pressure on resources, to make available essential goods and services for the really poor.

Unless a sincere attempt is made we will continue to bury the problem of poverty under the carpet and poverty abolition will be confined to efforts and talks in five star hotels by brain starved governments. Renunciation of too much enjoyment by all is a must.

The great Greek philosopher Aristotle said twenty-five centuries ago, "what the world needs is cleansing of hearts and not garments," Is this not true even today. We claim to have made lot of progress. Our science and technology have advanced. Our general economic condition has improved. We have more comforts and access to information from any corner of the globe. But with all these and many others, are we really happy? What have we done to improve the lot of the really poor people, exceeding one billion, who are unable to get even one square meal a day? They are not able to acquire minimum education. They don't have a roof over their heads. The have rags on their backs and empty bellies. When they fall sick they do not get the right medical care. Why they should be condemned to a life of penury and misery. Do we, the better off and fortunate among the citizens, have a responsibility to do something within our power to uplift these unfortunate masses?

Everywhere polluted minds exist. They spit venom and spread the contagion of misery and disaster. Even with the most powerful intellect we have not been able to overcome their evil effects. The mightiest nation has not been able to counter their evil designs. The calamity of 9/11 is an example.

Death and destruction in many parts of the globe have become the order of the day. There is wastage of resources. Priorities are lost sight of and in the name of economic development the poor are deprived of their essential requirements for want of resources, or infrastructure, or organizations. We make efforts here and there but they do not make any serious dent on the problem.

It seems there is rise of evil. This brings about competition and waste. Many organizations have a percentage of parasites that take more than what they give. They are more aware of their rights and not duties. Social commitments of organizations are inadequate. Poverty and oppression all over the world, except pockets of wealth and prosperity, do exist. So too is with ignorance and illiteracy.

There are various international funding agencies with programmes of poverty eradication but the impact on the poor is slow and negligible. We see countries with booming economy, creating billionaires but the poor live a miserable life as before. Is it not our duty to lift them up from the morass of poverty and despondency? The world economy by and large is greed driven and not by values. The disparity in wealth is increasing. But the large income accruing to the already rich do not find in deployment resources for the welfare of the poor. If the poor around us are in a state of utter want and discontent how can there be stability in society.

Men want to satisfy their wants. Economics deals with satisfaction of human wants. Over a period of time wants become desires and they multiply They are the indiscriminate offspring of the mind .When they are satisfied at the lowest level more and more desires and wants manifest and demand fulfillment. This becomes greed. The nature of greed and its growth is like pouring ghee into fire. The intensity becomes great. When resources are not available to satisfy greed, crooked methods are sought. Greed commands resources and this need not necessarily be based on priority. So resources are cornered by people who perpetuate and promote greed. Though we may call many of them entrepreneurs, many turn out to be thieves of society.

When the tendency to satisfy greed becomes predominant in society such a society adopts all means fair and foul to muster resources. This leads to extensive borrowing since own resources are found to be inadequate. Excessive borrowing creates a situation where repayment of loans becomes difficult and default occurs. This sets in motion a chain reaction and the economy collapses causing fall in employment and rise in economic misery. The lone culprit is greed.

Thus the bane of society is greed and if we want to improve society and its economic condition we must curb greed. Greed results in wastage of resources. The recent stock market crash and global meltdown confirm this phenomenon.

Recent global melt down had its origin in human greed which prompted individuals to acquire assets even at the risk of heavy borrowing. Banks welcomed borrowers to further their business. This led to business boom and later a bubble burst. We are yet to recover from the onslaught of this big hit. Share markets crashed. Banks collapsed .This resulted in loss of millions of jobs. Loss of income caused proliferation of misery. Economic theory based on multiplicity of desires and wants can only offer a faulty structure with loose foundation.

Are not resources cornered and wasted? Are there not priorities for human existence? Why not upgrade human values which will definitely scale down greed and ensure better standards of living for all instead of extreme happiness for a few and acute misery for many. Controlling greed is the function of controlling the mind with the power of the intellect. If our educational system can achieve this in a decade steadily we will definitely march towards stable progress without tears. Let us start building up a global value system relinquishing greed. Let us not salute greed as an engine of economic progress.

While greed dominates economic order, spiraling inflation demolishes the hopes of any progress for the poor. Disorder and discontent become their constant companions. There is unhappiness due to lack of essential things for their use. There is unhappiness for the rich due to a feeling of insecurity for the protection of their life and property. Is this state of tension, stress and anxiety desirable? How can we get over this?

How long should this continue?. Is it not time to end this? Efforts of several agencies like the World Bank, Asian Development Bank yield some results but they are inadequate.

What is the way out? The only way is to originate solutions from the heart of human beings. Where intellect fails the heart succeeds, the heart of the Buddha with overflowing compassion for the unfortunate ones. Out of that compassion springs forth spontaneous release of resources from individuals. This alone can solve the problem of poverty and misery. There will be less for governmental intervention. Let us fill every heart with values. This does not mean the present functions discharged by the governments should be discarded or given less importance. In addition make human hearts overflow with concern and compassion for releasing resources and energy for the uplift of the really poor. A civilization worth the name should really progress in cleansing the hearts. It is a heart full with values, which will be the springboard of love. Noble action and programmes for the uplift of the poor will follow. This needs a global view.

Poverty cannot be abolished by the efforts of persons who travel in executive class and live in five star hotel and comforts. They should really understand the problems of the poor. They should feel for them and live poverty at least for a while to understand the intensity of the malady. Human relationships should be based on love and helping the others. It should not be brushed aside as pure philosophy or impractical ideal. In fact the idealist is the most practical man in the world. He raises the level of practicality to the ideal and does not pull down the ideal to the low level of practicality. There is need for a supra ordinary goal of human welfare and happiness with focus on programmes for the really poor. We must go back to Gandhian values and our ancient wisdom which ensured social security without state intervention.

We have to mould a new generation if the present one cannot accomplish or attune to this. We should stop this plunder of resources by a section of rich and fortunate ones who in the name of progress are driven by greed instead of need. Programmes of education and skill development should tap the mental strength of mankind and tap the heart for the inexhaustible fountain of love. This alone can provide a lasting solution for world peace, prosperity, happiness and stability. This should be done with the full participation of the really poor that will benefit. Globalization of values is the need of the times. This is the task of global and national leadership. Our efforts during all these centuries have been the result of application of the intelligence to solve man's problems. But have we solved them fully? Are we confident that they will be solved with the intellect alone? Is there a better way open to us? It is here Aristotle's statement becomes more relevant today. Let us make a beginning now. Thus we can pay a glowing tribute to Aristotle and his maxim. Let us pray wisdom will dawn on our leaders who profess to be champions of poverty alleviation.

11. Talent and Poverty Alleviation

Progress is the function of good leadership and talents. Leaders should locate talents within their areas of responsibility and influence. This has to be a continuous process. The right leadership is welcomed by talented individual to make contributions to society. Sri Lanka has tried this talent hunt for poverty abolition and has succeeded. When society grows poverty recedes.

We all know what talent means. This is a natural skill or ability at something. It comes to people in diverse ways. Some people are lucky to live out the full potential of their talents; some others discover their talents but are not privileged enough to harness them; while yet another group live and die without ever knowing what their real talents are. In any community there will be at least one person who is very good in at least one activity. It might be somebody known to us or not.

Ideally we might hope that society would reward people having talent. The person with ability to do a particular activity would go on to use that ability to his and society's advantage. That is perfectly logical.

But often we find that people with talent are not allowed to use that talent and frustration develops. More than this society as a whole loses the advantages of having the best people employed in positions best suited to them.

A few examples are cited below:

This is a typical case where a young professionally qualified experienced entrepreneur, a law abiding citizen, has been financially ruined by the inaction of the government authorities. He is forced to flee his home country in search of livelihood after incurring heavy losses in the industry, with potential employment of over 100 workers, which commenced operations after fulfilling all rules and regulations. This is solely due to the versatile incompetence of those holding leadership positions in government. The government ordered levying dead rent for an area, which was not in actual possession (except on paper) of the talented entrepreneur.

The entrepreneur, a young business administration graduate, operated three granite quarries for a short period of 29 months. This was despite having a mining lease for ten years. There was absolutely no violation of rules and regulations of the departments concerned with mining under the State government.

The operation during this short period of 29 months was done successfully and a royalty of Rs. 1.80 crores paid to the government. The first quarry operations went on smoothly and substantial amount of royalty(Rs 1.35 crores) was paid to the government. In the second and third quarry, operations came to a standstill due to governmental inaction. So the royalty came to Rs 36 lakhs and Rs 9 lakhs respectively. Due to reasons beyond the control of the entrepreneur he was unable to work all the quarries after 29 months of granting lease and the mines remained idle through out the remaining years (9 years) of the lease period of 11 years. The operations could not be continued solely due to the hurdles imposed by the government officials, particularly at the district and village levels. The government did not respect facts while taking decisions affecting the entrepreneur, the employees and the industry. The allegations made by the people supported by various levels of leadership represented by the politicians, trade unions and the press were made with the only motive of blackmailing and extortion from a soft entrepreneur. Legal hurdles, public agitations and harassment backed by governmental lethargy and inaction froze further operations.

Dead rent is that levied for the period when there is no mining activity. This was demanded based on erroneous calculation, and was discriminatory. This apart, the original demand of Rs 18 lakhs was raised to Rs 40.5 lakhs ignoring the fact that the entrepreneur had no *physical possession* of the leased area, (except on document). He was unable to get access to the area for mining due to the obstructions caused by the local people supported by others and the government officials issuing faulty, orders oblivious of precedents followed by the State, and high courts. The government had no authority to demand dead rent in view of the high court rulings and its own precedents in disposing of similar cases relating to dead rent. The judgments of the high courts and the orders of the Ministry and government's precedents clearly stated that dead rent was not payable for such periods when the lessee had no actual physical possession of the mining land and had to suspend operations due to reasons beyond his control.

The entrepreneur, consequent to governmental inaction and failure to award justice, incurred huge losses, unproductive and avoidable expenses including court expenses. He had heavy borrowings. In the absence of operations, he lost skilled labor, disbanded sophisticated machinery and forced by legal and government's hurdles, went bankrupt.

The officials handling the cases of the victim did not have up-to-date knowledge of even orders issued by them earlier and of court decisions by various high courts according to which levy of dead rent was not justified. The entrepreneur goaded by his dogged determination to collect facts relating to the cases handled by the judiciary in other states, and the governments, made sincere efforts to educate the officials concerned presenting the facts. But their inability to see through facts and to draw right conclusions resulted in disastrous decision and consequences to him.

There was no damage to the environment from quarrying and the experts in the field had verified and certified this. Yet operations had to be discontinued due to public pressure and obstruction. The government agencies, which refused to obey the directions of the court order, which specifically said that, no valid grounds existed for stopping operations. With threat to life of the lessee and his workmen the very approach to the leased area itself was blocked.

Despite persistent efforts to educate the government officials by presenting facts and orders issued by their own departments and the judiciary, the promoter was not awarded equitable justice. His complaints to the Head of the Administration, Police and the appellate authority were dismissed.

There was no lapse on the part of the entrepreneur in meeting his obligations to the public, government or to the department. He had reported the matter to the authorities. The geologist after inspection of the quarries appeared before the court and defended the entrepreneur disapproving the contentions of those who caused physical obstruction preventing entry to the mines.

These facts definitely affirmed the fact that the entrepreneur though had legal possession of the leased mine, had no physical possession and could not operate the mines. The Courts, clearly made exemptions from levy of such rent where there was no physical possession of the mining land by the lessee. There was no justification for levying dead rent which was as silly as the justification for levying rent for the use of the sky when no aircraft was permitted to fly

.Ignorance of law is no excuse. How to deal with such leaders in the governmental hierarchy? Should they be dealt with in full compliance of the provisions of the law for negligence and dereliction of duty and causing undue harassment and mental torture to a young qualified entrepreneur forcing him to abandon his business and flee the country for his livelihood? Can there be a better example of officials playing the role of brand ambassadors of versatile incompetence. Thus the flight of talent from a country to a foreign country where talent is respected and rewarded took place. This should not happen if we want to eliminate poverty.

In another case young boys work part time for large maintenance companies. Their job is to clean houses prior to the new home owner occupies. One such boy working is excellent at his job and to our surprise we discover that he works at the job full time and has a M.Sc in Mathematics. Here is a brilliant fellow who could have easily made an excellent mathematics teacher or a manager now working as a cleaner. Something went wrong there. One might say he was happy .But the society lost his services for a better contribution.

A very poor student who is unable to complete his education due to the lack of financial resources has the talent to go all the way to a PhD or D.Sc but money stops him at high school or at their first degree. What a waste. Every year many brilliant students are prevented from achieving their potential because of lack of finance.

Government policies are very strong instruments of change. The change can either be productive or destructive depending on the accompanying variables. The issue of skills acquisition is not known to have been taken seriously by our governments. You can hardly find any creativity centre run by government anywhere in the country. The ones initiated by private individuals complain of lack of government patronage.

We need good economy to harness creative talents and we need harnessed talents to create good economy. We have to develop a synergy between the already developed talents and the government in order to harness more talents. Society should learn from the mistakes of that generation that mismanaged creativity and do better

There are many young men and women in our society today who need capital to launch one enterprise or the other. There should be a synergy between the government and philanthropists to empower creative youths.

Leaders at various levels should take seriously such projects as job centers, creativity village, skill acquisition, and organizations that promote creativity. These, shall in turn contribute to build a strong and stable economy where creative empowerment and social development will be a way of life. We must learn to discover and promote creative talents wherever they are.

12. Eclipse of Poverty

Anti poverty measures call for immediate action. Our emphasis is on leadership development which we have discussed in some detail in earlier chapters. Action by leadership in power, in the opposition, the people within the country and by the rich nations is necessary. This is summarized below.

Leadership in Power

1. Set up a *Ministry for Poverty Alleviation*

2. Consider impact of action taken under various schemes in favour of organised sections on unorganised sections of labour
3. Create a well integrated power network based on systems approach
4. Create opportunities for employment
5. Develop power management objectives
6. Develop problem solving approach
7. Discard craze for privileges
8. Discourage problem creating leaders
9. Do not make promises and rapidly wear them out
10. Encourage enterprise and talent
11. Encourage productive employment
12. Firmly maintain law and order
13. Focus attention on areas of immediate returns i.e., prioritising needs of the people, strengthening law and order base and rooting out corruption
14. Give up the implicit policy of being a soft state
15. Improve quality of life
16. Inculcate discipline
17. Look constantly for disruption in power structure and take corrective action
18. Manage power effectively

19. Motivate people
20. Realize the power potential of the administration
21. Reduce inequality of opportunity
22. Set clear anti-poverty objectives
23. Use tax system as a motivating tool

Opposition
1. Hold on to anti-poverty objectives
2. Help government to realize anti poverty objectives
3. Do not disrupt the power structure
4. Do not stifle enterprise
5. Do not stall legislative proceedings
6. Impart discipline and decorum in dealings
7. Do not demoralize those working for increased output, productivity and employment
8. Do not constrict opportunity
9. Do not cause wastage of resources by encouraging breakdown of law and order
10. Do not disrupt value systems
11. Give up problem creating approach
12. Improve quality of life

The People

1. Choose right leaders who will deliver positive results
2. Develop individual objectives consistent with national objectives

Rich Nations

1. Be pace setters in simpler ways of living
2. Create infrastructure in group of villages with stress on generating quality leadership
3. Ensure sustainability of resources
4. Focus assistance on education
5. Promote development leadership;

6. Set anti poverty objective in the world context
7. Step up contributing to poverty alleviation programmes

In addition to action on these lines the state has to change its role. Its function should be to create opportunities for improving the quality of life of citizens.

Poverty is a painful experience. It arises from many causes, the most important being poverty of right leadership. This has been attested by great world leaders. There is considerable scope for improvement through clear anti poverty objectives which also require leadership objectives. This requires effective 'power management'. The role of power is to motivate the people and not to regulate their freedom indiscriminately curbing initiative and enterprise. Rich nations can render considerable help by providing assistance for development leadership. We can learn a lot from countries like Sri Lanka in the area of poverty alleviation and leadership development.

Democracy should not mean a surfeit of freedom for the leaders and people to do anything they like so that 'the horse begins to drive the wayfarer from the road'. What the country in particular and the world in general need today is *cleansing of hearts and not of garments.* Emphasis should be laid on character development which is a highly productive intangible asset. Such an approach to the nation's problems by the leaders and the lead will pave the way for the elimination of poverty. There is enough for our present day leaders in all walks of life to learn from our ancient scriptures, which have as much relevance today as it was in the distant past.

Our vision in India is to make India a great place to work. Such a lofty vision cannot be achieved by a group of mediocre, uninspired individuals posing as leaders. The sheer magnitude of the vision makes it necessary that we attract inspired people who are not just talented in the ordinary sense of having outstanding competencies, but deeply passionate about making a difference. Such a leadership alone can cure poverty.

***

Appendix

Sri Lanka's Experience

Sri Lanka analyzed the reasons for the failure of earlier programmes. The analysis revealed that there was no long term vision, too much freedom, lack of social discipline, futility of giving everything free of charge, and the danger of working on wrong paradigms and conflicting policies.

The country identified some important indicators of poverty. These were low income, hunger, low education, gender, shelter and poor infrastructure. It launched the *prosperity movement* in line with the millennium development goal declared in 2000. These goals were clear and *people centered* for all agencies involved in development. This included the government, citizens, private sector, international organizations Community Service Organizations. The Government set up a *Ministry of Prosperity (*Samurdhi).Poverty indices district wise were prepared to give direction to the effort needed.

The Government set eight goals. These were

1. Eradicate extreme poverty and hunger
2. Achieve universal primary education
3. Promote gender equality and empower women
4. Reduce child mortality

5. Improve maternal health`
6. Combat HIV/AIDS, malaria and other diseases
7. Ensure environmental sustainability
8. Develop global partnership for development

For each goal thus determined the Government set targets e.g., halve extreme poverty and hunger by 2015

Youth and Cultural Development was set up as a new division of the authority. The objective was to alleviate poverty through youth development (empowerment), vocational training, talent identification and development, organising the youth and provide knowledge, information, attitude and skills

The Prosperity Movement (Samurdhi) had a very clear vision, mission, goals, objectives and strategies.
The vision statement was:

Prosperous Sri Lanka with minimized poverty

The benefits of the Prosperity (Samurdhi) Movement are:

Employment of village based Change Agents who work hard to empower the poor and graduate them out of the poverty trap.
The vast network of the Samurdhi Movement is used more effectively and efficiently through pro-poor approaches.
The original concept was designed and developed by S.B. Dissanayake, who was the Minister of Samurdhi, He provided the *leadership* and now it has grown into a massive organization with a national network of community based organizations and public administration network.

This reflects on the high caliber of leadership and the chain of leaders who worked with the will to succeed.

About 26,000 full-timers were engaged as "Change Agents" of the movement. 24,000 Samurdhi Development Officers and 2,000 graduate managers covered about 2,000,000 families

The mission objective was to contribute to national development through empowerment and graduation of the low-income people out of poverty line and reduce disparity in their livelihood in the manner of participatory development through the process of *identification and development of innate abilities* of the low income families.

The major achievements are formal & informal organizational structure. Samurdhi Movement is a combination of formal & informal structures.

The formal structure consists of The Ministry, Departments, Authority, District Secretaries, Divisional Secretaries, Areas, Village Vasama, Ministry of Samurdhi Programme, Poor Relief Dept. (subsidy programme) Samurdhi Authority Empowerment and Development programme

Samurdhi Commissioners department covers all insurance and infrastructure development.

Formal structure exists at National, Provisional District, Divisional, Grama vasama, Village levels with

4 million families.

Informal structure consists of family level 2 million families, each of 5 member group, Samurdhi society- village level, Area society- area level, General union,-district level and National level (poor people's parliament)

Major programmes undertaken were social welfare, social insurance, infrastructure development, micro credit, income generation and socio-cultural development. Social Insurance Programme was implemented by Samurdhi Commissioner's Department which deducted Rs. 30 from the subsidy and the beneficiaries were entitled to receive following financial benefit depending on the occasion or event.

Death – Rs. 5,000

Wedding – Rs. 3,000

Child birth – Rs. 2,000

Hospitalization – Rs. 1,500 (Rs.50 x 30 days)

Educational Scholarship Programme for above poverty line students.-6,000 students were getting this benefit.

Rural development division alleviated poverty through youth development (empowerment) vocational training, talent identification and development, organising the youth and provide knowledge, information, attitude and skills.

Social Development Division undertook anti - smoking, alcohol, and drug prevention programme, reducing Illiteracy programme, suicide prevention and reduction programme

Anti smoking flag day – housing development for acute poor (Rs. 18 million in 2002 for 2000 houses), child care and widow mother development (specially trained 450 SDOs were engaged. Socio-cultural development, social development, human resource development, youth & cultural development programmes were implemented.

Cost & Benefit of the Change Agents are given below:

Total Cost of SDOs & SMs

28,000 x Rs.10, 000 = Rs. 280,000,000

If one officer can graduate 10 families out-of

poverty trap by improving their income up-to

Rs.3, 000 a month the total benefit will be 26,000

x 10 x Rs. 3,000 = Rs.780, 000,000

If 200,000 families' income can be improved up-to

Rs. 3,000 per month then = Rs.600, 000,000

If 100,000 families' income can be improved up-to

Rs. 3,000 per month then = Rs. 300,000,000.

Source:

Poverty Alleviation in Sri Lanka:
With special reference to Samurdhi
(Prosperity) Movement

By

Sunil Jayantha Nawaratne

Professor of Management & E-Commerce
Sri Lanka Institute of Information Technology
Chairman
Centre for Strategic Management

Bibliography

Books

- Life of Swami Vivekananda, Ramakrishna Mission, Kolkata
- Wikipedia- Poverty in India
- Poverty in India- Economy Watch
- UNDP Human Development Report 2010
- Planning Commission of India, Poverty Estimates for 2004-05
- Wikipedia, the free encyclopedia
- Education the Cure for Poverty? | The American Prospect
- Wealth & Poverty of Nations (Paperback) by David S. Landes
- Publisher: Hachette Book Publishing India (01/07/99)
- A Farewell to Alms: A Brief Economic History of the World (Princeton Economic History of the Western World) [Paperback]
- Developing Poverty: The State, Labor Market Deregulation, and the Informal Economy in Costa Rica and the Dominican Republic [Paperback]
- The End of Poverty: Economic Possibilities for Our Time (ISBN 1-59420-045-9) is a 2005 book by American economist Jeffrey Sachs
- The Bottom Billion: Why the Poorest Countries are Failing and What Can Be Done About It is a 2007 book by Paul Collier, Professor of Economics at Oxford University,
- K. L. Datta and S. Sharma: Facets of Indian Poverty, Concept Publishing Company, New Delhi, 2002, pp. xxi + 175, Rs.120, ISBN: 81-7022959-6
- The Nature of Mass Poverty [1] is an economics book by John Kenneth Galbraith published in 1979. ^ ISBN 0-674-60533-0 Originally given as lectures at the Graduate Institute of International Studies, University of Geneva and at Radcliffe Institute;

- Progress and Poverty was written by Henry George in 1879. The book is a treatise on the cyclical nature of an industrial economy
- Understanding Poverty [Paperback]
- Pete Alcock (Author) 2006
- Poverty (Key Concepts) [Paperback]
- Ruth Lister2004
- Poverty and Social Exclusion in Britain: The Millennium Survey (Studies in Poverty, Inequality & Social Exclusion) [Paperback]
- Dave Gordon (Editor), Ruth Levitas (Editor), Christina Pantazis (Editor 2006
- No-nonsense Guide to World Poverty (No-Nonsense Guides) [Paperback]
- Jeremy Seabrook 2007
- Understanding Inequality, Poverty and Wealth: Policies and Prospects (Understanding Welfare: Social Issues, Policy & Practice) [Illustrated] [Paperback]
- Tess Ridge (Author, Editor), Sharon Wright (Editor) 2008
- The Wealth and Poverty of Nations [Paperback]
- David S. Landes (Author) 1999
- Creating a World Without Poverty: Social Business and the Future of Capitalism [Paperback]
- Muhammad Yunus
- Muhammad Yunus (Author) 2009
- Poverty and Development [Paperback]
- Tim Allen (Editor), Alan Thomas (Editor 2000
- India: Urban Poverty Report 2009   Author(s): Ministry of Housing and Urban Poverty Alleviation and UNDP
- 9780198060253, Paperback
- February 2009
- Chronic Poverty and Development Policy in India
- Author: Mehta, Aasha Kapur & Shepherd, Andrew
- Year: 2006
- ISBN: 0761934642

- Poverty, Food Security and Sustainability: Public Distribution System in India
- Bhaskar Majumder, Rawat, 2004, 216 p, tables, ISBN: 81-7033-870-0
- 2020- A Vision for the New Millennium
- APJ Abdul Kalam With YS Rajan
- Published By: Penguin Books India (Private) Limited, New Delhi.

Web sites
- www.indianchild.com
- Poverty in India www.worldbank.org
- en.wikipedia.org/wiki/Poverty
- www.globalissues.org/article/4/poverty
- www.worldbank.org/poverty
- www.answers.com/topic/poverty
- world-poverty.org/solutionstopoverty.aspx
- www.globalissues.org/issue/2/causes-of-poverty
- www.newworldencyclopedia.org/entry/Poverty
- www.cgdev.org/section/topics/poverty
- www.prospect.org/cs/articles?article=is_education_the_cure_for_poverty
- www.americanthinker.com/blog/2009/03/the_cure_for_poverty_1.html
- wdfavour.com/the-cure-for-poverty
- thecureforpoverty.com
- www.facebook.com/notes/st-louis-staffing/the-cure-for-poverty/188982270055
- www.thefreemanonline.org/columns/the-cure-for-poverty
- itunes.apple.com/us/podcast/the-cure-for-poverty/id360873223
- wiki.answers.com/Q/Is_education_the_cure_for_poverty
- www.ummah.com/forum/showthread.php?2125-Capitalism-The-Cure-for-Poverty

Articles

- Limits to Growth The Economic Times Annual 1972
- Process of Growth- The Economic Times Annual 1972
- Leadership Beyond Boundaries: Poverty - A Leadership Dilemma
- http://leadbeyond.org
- leadbeyond.blogspot.com/2009/02/poverty-leadership-dilemma.html

- leadershiplearning.org/taxonomy/term/68
- www.combarriers.com/Leadership ·
- Poverty and Leadership Part 3 -
- content.msn.co.in/MSNContribute/Story.aspx?PageID=56da1ece-76a2-4d2b-8329-0b24309cfac8 ·
- Poverty Of Leadership – Forward.com
- povertynewsblog.blogspot.com/2008/04/lamido-blames-poverty-on-leadership.html
- ezinearticles.com/? Connection-Between-African-Leadership-and-Poverty &id=3828771

www.ingramcontent.com/pod-product-compliance
Lightning Source LLC
Chambersburg PA
CBHW051213170526
45166CB00005B/1884

*9 7 8 1 5 2 2 7 2 5 9 9 2 *